TO _____

FROM _____

DATE _____

Published by Christian Art Publishers
PO Box 1599, Vereeniging, 1930, RSA

© 2022
First edition 2022

Devotions adapted from *What Would Jesus Do?*
© 1998 by Christian Art Publishers

Cover designed by Christian Art Publishers

Designed by Christian Art Publishers

Images used under license from Shutterstock.com

Unless otherwise indicated, all Scripture quotations are taken
from the Holy Bible, New International Version®, NIV®
Copyright © 1973, 1978, 1984 by Biblica, Inc.®
Used by permission. All rights reserved worldwide.

Scripture quotations marked NLT are taken from the Holy Bible,
New Living Translation, copyright © 1996, 2004, 2015 by Tyndale
House Foundation. Used by permission of Tyndale House
Publishers, Carol Stream, Illinois 60188.
All rights reserved.

Set in 13 on 15 pt Cronos Pro by Christian Art Publishers

Printed in China

ISBN 978-1-77637-076-4

© All rights reserved. No part of this book may be reproduced
in any form without permission in writing from the publisher,
except in the case of brief quotations in critical articles or reviews.

22 23 24 25 26 27 28 29 30 31 – 10 9 8 7 6 5 4 3 2 1

Printed in Shenzhen, China
OCTOBER 2021
Print Run: PUR401923

ONE-MINUTE DEVOTIONS®

for

Kids

JAN DE WET

CHRISTIAN ART
PUBLISHERS

THE NEW YEAR

This is the day the LORD has made; let us rejoice and be glad in it. (Psalm 118:24)

It always feels good to start something new. It feels good to wear new shoes or to ride a new bicycle. You are most probably in a new grade this year with new challenges waiting for you.

If you put your hand in Jesus' hand, then He will lead you safely this new year, every step of the way. He says in His Word that every day is the day of the Lord and that it is a gift.

Come, let's be joyful and happy about every new day, and also about this new year that the Lord has given us. Let's ask the Lord to bless us and to help us do only what is important to Him. With Him to lead us this will be a wonderful year.

WINNERS FOR JESUS

But thanks be to God, who always leads us in triumphal procession in Christ.
(2 Corinthians 2:14)

When your school's team wins a sports match, it feels good to be on the winning side.

Just like on the sports field, there are also winners in life. Paul writes that we are running the race of life. This means how we live will determine whether we win or lose. The Bible tells us that if we live with Christ and give our lives to Him, then we are in the winning team. Jesus is the Great Winner. He paid for our sins on the cross and rose from the dead: He overcame death and the devil!

Decide to put your hand in Jesus' hand right now. Take on the rest of this day as a winner with Him. And if you have a problem or something hurtful happens today, leave it in Jesus' hands.

IS GOD DEAD?

The fool says in his heart, "There is no God."
(Psalm 14:1)

Many people say that God is dead. Some think He doesn't exist, some say He has retired, others that He is asleep or is not interested in people. Maybe they feel that way because they cannot see or touch Him.

The Bible says that someone who thinks this is a fool. They are making a big mistake. One day a man came up to a pastor and told him that God does not exist. The pastor responded, "But that's impossible; just this morning I spoke to Him and He to me!"

If you really believe in God, you just know, deep down, that the Lord truly lives. He talks to you through His Word, and you can talk to Him in prayer. Then you know that He exists and lives in your heart.

Does God live in your heart?

STARTING ALL OVER AGAIN

One thing I do: Forgetting what is behind and straining toward what is ahead.
(Philippians 3:13)

We all make mistakes. The worst part is that sometimes you make the same mistake over and over again! If you keep on thinking of past mistakes, you can start feeling depressed.

But the Bible tells us if we have made a mistake and we are sorry about it, we must tell the Lord. And once we have confessed our sin, the Lord forgives us immediately. Then He doesn't think about it again.

Paul says that he will put everything that happened in the past behind him. He will look ahead and try to live the way he should. Tell the Lord that you are sorry about the mistakes you made in the past, thank Him for forgiving you, and live to the full every moment of this new day.

LAUGH AND CRY

Rejoice with those who rejoice; mourn with those who mourn. (Romans 12:15)

I'm sure you have sometimes had a good laugh about something that happened to you. But then again, you have also cried a lot about things that made you sad.

God says we must laugh with those who laugh and cry with those who cry. When people are happy, we must also be happy because we love people and care for them. If someone hurts and cries, we must cry with them, because we don't like to see others hurting.

If the love of God is in our hearts, we want to feel what others feel. If you know of a friend who is unhappy, go and tell him or her that you are sorry about it. If something good happens, tell him or her that you are happy for them.

I'LL SHOW YOU

Do not take revenge, my friends, but leave room for God's wrath. (Romans 12:19)

Has anyone ever hurt you or upset you? Often people do things that make us very angry and we want to pay them back. We feel like saying, "I'll show you!" Then some guys start fighting, using either their fists or their tongues.

The Bible says this is not a wise thing to do. It is much better to forgive each other. And if we still feel in our hearts that the other person must be paid back, we should ask God to do it. He is a fair Judge. At the end of our lives each one of us will stand before the great throne of God. Then God will pass judgment (Romans 2:3).

Forgive any friend that hurt you. Do it right now, and then leave it in God's hands.

GO TO GOD

Since we have confidence to enter the Most Holy Place by the blood of Jesus, let us draw near to God with a sincere heart in full assurance of faith. (Hebrews 10:19, 22)

Many people are afraid to go to God. Maybe because they think He won't understand how they feel or that He's strict and just wants to judge and punish them.

This is not true! God loves us so much that He gave us His Son. When Jesus died for us on the cross, the curtain of the temple tore from top to bottom. Since that time, we can talk to Him every day and anywhere.

He knows everything you do and say, and He is with you every moment of the day. It's all right to take all your problems to Him and to talk to Him about everything that happens to you. He understands and He loves you.

EVERY KNEE WILL BOW

That in the name of Jesus every knee should bow ... and every tongue confess that Jesus Christ is Lord. (Philippians 2:10, 11)

The Bible says that everyone in heaven and on earth, and even under the earth, will kneel before Jesus Christ. This means that everybody will confess that He is the Savior, the only One who can free us from sin and bring us salvation.

In biblical times, subjects of the king bowed before him to show that he was greater and more powerful than they were. That is why everyone will also bow to King Jesus one day.

If you accept Jesus as your Savior, then you bow before Him in your heart and you confess that He has become your King. Then you want to live for Him and do what He wants you to. Have you kneeled before Him yet?

WORK OUT THE COST

"Suppose one of you wants to build a tower. Will he not first sit down and estimate the cost to see if he has enough money to complete it?" (Luke 14:28)

Before you can buy something you want badly, you must first see if you have enough money.

The Bible says there is also a price to pay if we want to follow Jesus. It will cost us something very precious to know that we will be with Him in heaven forever: our hearts. We say to Him, "Here is my heart, take it; I have decided to follow You." And if there are people who do not like it if I follow Jesus or tease me because I say that I love Jesus, then that is the price I must pay for the joy of being His child.

But, you know, it is always a bargain to follow Jesus.

CHARGE YOUR BATTERY

"God rested on the seventh day. Therefore the LORD blessed the Sabbath day and made it holy." (Exodus 20:11)

Batteries are useful. New batteries make a flashlight shine brightly, or make a toy car go. But batteries also go dead. Like batteries, we humans also get tired. Then we cannot do our work properly, and we don't feel good.

Because God knows this, He set aside one day a week so that we can rest. If we work hard every day of the week, then we need to rest over weekends. But we must also rest spiritually. Our hearts must be tuned in to hear God's voice and to do what He asks.

We can enjoy resting in God's presence by going to church, listening to His Word, and singing songs with His other children. In this way we charge the batteries of our lives.

THE SPECK AND THE PLANK

"First take the plank out of your own eye, and then you will see clearly to remove the speck from your brother's eye."
(Matthew 7:5)

A plank is a long, flat piece of wood used for making floors and framing houses. A speck is so tiny you can hardly see it. We all have our faults, and sometimes these faults are so big that they are like a thick plank in our eye. But we pretend not to notice. We like telling others how big their sins and faults are, but we are not honest about our own.

Jesus says we should not blame others. It is much better to first take care of our own faults and take the thick plank of sin out of our own eyes. Even better than that is not to find fault with others at all, just love them with their faults.

TRAIN, TRAIN, TRAIN

Train yourself to be godly.
(1 Timothy 4:7, NLT)

If you want to play the piano well, you have to practice a lot. Athletes must also train hard and learn the rules of their sport so that they can be good at it.

It is not always easy to train or practice for something, but you do it anyway because you know that it will help you do better. It is the same with schoolwork: if you work hard, you get good grades in tests or exams.

The Bible says if we want to learn how to live successfully, we must also train ourselves in our relationship with God. This means we have to read the Bible regularly, talk to God, and do things that will help us in our relationship with Him. Just like an athlete trains, we must make time for God every day.

Will you do this today?

THE THIRSTY DEER

As the deer pants for streams of water, so my soul pants for You, O God. (Psalm 42:1)

If you visit a game reserve or state park, you will notice how far deer must walk to get to water. In biblical times, the deer in the desert also had to walk long distances to get to water.

This is how the Bible explains that people are also thirsty for the water that only God can give us. Jesus said He is the Fountain of Living Water. His love is like a cool stream of water we can drink from to quench the thirst in our hearts.

We drink God's water as we listen when He speaks to us through His Word, and we are filled with the Holy Spirit. Why not tell the Lord right now that you are drinking His Living Water so that you may never be thirsty again?

A WONDERFUL INVITATION

"Follow Me and be My disciple," Jesus said to him. (Matthew 9:9)

Matthew was most probably a very rich man. He had a booth where people had to pay tax money. Often the tax collectors took more money than they were supposed to, and so they became very rich.

One day Jesus saw Matthew sitting at his booth, and said to him, "Follow Me!" Maybe Matthew was surprised at this invitation, but what is even more surprising is that he immediately left everything and started following Jesus. Amazing!

Perhaps the love in Jesus' eyes made up Matthew's mind. Perhaps Matthew had a longing for peace deep in his heart that only Jesus could give. Perhaps Matthew realized that only Jesus could free him from sin.

Jesus has invited you to follow Him. Give Him your whole life!

RUN AWAY

Joseph tore himself away, but he left his cloak in her hand as he ran from the house.
(Genesis 39:12, NLT)

Joseph loved God very much, and God had a wonderful plan for Joseph's life. Although Joseph's brothers sold him as a slave, God was with him. Joseph worked for Potiphar, an important man in the palace of Pharaoh, Egypt's leader.

Potiphar's evil wife wanted Joseph to do wrong. He refused and ran away from her, and she ended up only grabbing his coat. Later on she told lies about Joseph, but God helped him.

It is always better to run away from people who want you to do something sinful. If you know it is wrong, say no, as Joseph did. If they don't want to listen, it is better to walk or run away. Even if they think you're a coward, the Lord will be on your side.

SEVENTY-SEVEN TIMES

"Lord, how often should I forgive someone who sins against me? Seven times?" "No, not seven times," Jesus replied, "but seventy times seven! (Matthew 18:21-22, NLT)

Sometimes it is so difficult to forgive, especially if someone has hurt us or made us angry. We would much rather get back at them than forgive them.

But the Bible says that the best thing to do is to forgive someone for what they have done. And not just once. We must be prepared to forgive each another up to seventy times seven. That's a lot! Actually, the number seven is the perfect number in the Bible, so Jesus wants us to forgive perfectly or completely. Even if someone sins against me three thousand times, in the same way, I must keep on forgiving.

Is there someone you need to forgive? Why not tell God right now that you forgive that person?

WONDERFULLY MADE

I praise You because I am fearfully and wonderfully made. (Psalm 139:14)

Just think how many people there are on earth. Every person looks different, talks differently, and acts in a different way. Isn't it wonderful?

Some people have black hair, others are blond; some are tall, others are short; some are fat, others are skinny. Every person is unique and special. You too! You are wonderfully made. Maybe you don't think you're very pretty, or maybe you can't run as fast as somebody you know. Maybe you can't sing. But it doesn't matter, because you are special. God gave you something that nobody else has.

Don't try to be like someone else. God made you unique. Just be yourself. Then God can use you, and you will also be happy. Won't you thank Him right now for making you so special and unique?

FEELING MISERABLE?

Hope deferred makes the heart sick.
(Proverbs 13:12, NLT)

When I was small, our family planned a wonderful holiday at a resort. We talked it over and dreamed about it, and we were so excited when the holidays finally came. But then something happened and we couldn't go anymore. I felt miserable.

Often, things don't work out the way we plan. Sometimes everything seems to go wrong at the same time and we can't help feeling depressed. Fortunately, God knows everything, and if you are His child, you can trust Him to help you. Through His Holy Spirit He helps and comforts us. Many times He assures us that there will be another opportunity.

If you are feeling miserable about something, leave it in Jesus' hands. He understands. Also, thank Him for the things that you do have. It will make you feel better.

LOT'S WIFE LOSES EVERYTHING

But Lot's wife looked back, and she became a pillar of salt. (Genesis 19:26)

Lot and his wife lived in Sodom. The people there would not do what God told them. So God decided to destroy Sodom. But because He loved Abraham, and Lot was part of Abraham's family, God warned Lot to flee. Lot's wife, however, did not want to leave all her nice things behind. When she looked back at Sodom, she turned into a pillar of salt, and she lost her life along with her possessions.

We must never love things more than God. He will look after us if we make Him King in our lives. Of course some things are very precious to us. But Jesus is much more precious.

One day, when we go to Him, we will have to leave everything behind anyway. Let's make Jesus number one in our lives right now.

FOOD WITHOUT SALT

"You are the salt of the earth."
(Matthew 5:13)

When we eat, we sprinkle salt onto the food. Salt gives food a better taste. Jesus said we, His children, are the salt of the earth. Like salt, we must flavor everything around us with our words and everything we do. People must enjoy having us around.

Today we use ointments and disinfectants to clean wounds. But in the old days they rubbed salt into wounds to get germs out and make them heal quickly. We, as children of God, must sometimes be like salt in the wounds of others. With our words and our actions we must help heal people's wounds.

If there is evil around us, we must overcome evil with good. For example, if someone swears, we should help him or her to see it is wrong.

ARE YOU A TREE?

They will be called oaks of righteousness.
(Isaiah 61:3)

An oak tree grows tall and wide. It is a lovely tree with many branches and bright green leaves. In summer one can take a rest in the shade of an oak tree. Birds also like building their nests in oak trees.

Isaiah says that you and I are like these trees – oaks that stand tall and proud. When people look at us they must also be able to say that we are just as upright as oak trees. What the Bible actually says is that you and I, because we are saved and belong to Jesus, stand up straight like the oak: a tree of righteousness. As children of the Lord, we are like big, beautiful oaks.

When people look at you today they must see an oak tree standing tall.

LIGHT IS STRONGER

The light shines in the darkness, and the darkness can never extinguish it.
(John 1:5, NLT)

In the dark it is very difficult to see where you are going. You can bump into things and hurt yourself. That is why we use a flashlight or switch on a light so that we can see. Light is stronger than darkness. The moment you switch on a light, the darkness disappears.

The Bible says that Jesus is the light that came into this world. He is like a bright light that drives out the darkness. And what is the darkness? It is the devil's influence. The devil is also called the prince of darkness.

The work of the devil is just as dim as the darkest night. Jesus came to change the darkness of the devil into light.

LOVE BUILDS

Be humble, thinking of others as better than yourselves. (Philippians 2:3, NLT)

When we really love someone, we do not want to hurt that person's feelings. We want to make that person happy. Paul writes in 1 Corinthians 13 that love does not always demand its own way. This means we want to build, or uplift, our loved ones and want what's best for them.

Uplifting someone is the opposite of criticizing that person. When we humiliate people, we make them feel small, which is wrong. Let's try to uplift those around us with our actions and especially with our words and our love. This will mean that you and I must encourage friends and other people and say something like, "Well done; that was good." Or, "You tried your best. If you keep trying like this, you will be a winner."

Let's build one another up in love.

GOD, OUR FATHER

"Our Father in heaven ... " (Matthew 6:9)

Jesus taught us how to pray. When we pray, we talk to God. We open our hearts to Him and tell Him everything that we think is important in our lives.

But before we can really pray, we need to have a personal relationship with God. This means that we must not feel that God is far away, but that He is close to us, because Jesus introduced us to Him. If we have worked out things between God and ourselves – because we accepted Jesus' offer on the cross – then the Almighty God becomes our Father.

The Bible also says the person who has the Son has life; but those who don't, don't have life. If you have accepted Jesus, God is also your Father. Therefore you may call Him Father. Then you can pray together with all Christians, "Our Father in heaven ... "

A WONDERFUL DAD

"To all who received Him, to those who believed in His name, He gave the right to become children of God." (John 1:12)

God is the Father of Jesus Christ. But He also becomes our Dad if we accept Him in faith. God wants us to be His children. But not everybody on earth is God's child; only those who have accepted Him. Are you God's child yet?

If you become God's child, you soon find out that He is a wonderful Father. Because He loves us so much and wants only the best for us, we must feel free to speak to Him and to hear Him as He talks to us through His Word.

He comforts and helps us through the Holy Spirit that He gave us. Yes, He is a wonderful Dad. Because He understands, and loves you, speak to Him today.

LOOKING FORWARD TO HEAVEN

"Our Father in heaven ... " (Matthew 6:9)

We don't really know where heaven is or what it looks like. What we do know is that it's a wonderful place. There are no tears, heartache or pain there. God lives in heaven with His Son, Jesus, and also with millions of angels that praise and serve Him all the time.

God rules in heaven and there is no sin to hurt people. Also, there isn't room for the devil. He lives in hell. Heaven is a joyful place, and nothing will make us sad or upset there. We will be able to see God and live forever without getting sick or old.

When God has become our Father, then we know for sure that there will be a place for us in heaven. Jesus went there to prepare our place. Do you look forward to heaven? How about speaking to your Father in heaven right now?

HIS NAME IS HOLY

" ... may Your name be kept holy."
(*Matthew 6:9, NLT*)

God has many names, like Father, Almighty, Immanuel, Jesus and King. All these names tell us more about Him, who He is, and how He acts.

Because God can never sin, all His names are beautiful and show His holiness. To be holy is to be pure and without sin. God's name is holy. That is why it really is terrible when people use His name carelessly, and even as a swear word. You must never do it. If you hear one of your friends doing it, you must, in a nice way, tell them that you love Jesus and that His name is holy.

When we pray, we say, " ... may Your name be kept holy." This means, "May Your name be just as wonderful and lovely as You, Lord." And when His name comes from our lips, then we speak with respect.

GOD'S KINGDOM

"May Your Kingdom come soon."
(Matthew 6:10, NLT)

In the past, many countries were ruled by a king or queen. They ruled over their land, and that was their kingdom, or domain. Today many countries have presidents or prime ministers instead.

The most important kingdom of all is the kingdom of God. You might ask, "Where is God's land?" Well, we could say it is in heaven, but it is also on earth. God does not have a piece of land like, say, America or Italy. His land or kingdom is everywhere that people accept His kingship. If you love the Lord and want to serve Him, then He is your King. Then your heart becomes His kingdom. And wherever you might be, you take His kingdom with you. Let's make Him King in our country and also of the whole world.

YOUR WILL OR HIS WILL?

"May Your will be done on earth."
(Matthew 6:10, NLT)

God rules in heaven, and there His will is done. What He says is done. His will is always best. He is like a good government that only wants what's best for its citizens.

The devil also has a will, and he always wants to get everybody to do his will. If we do what the devil wants, then we are asking for trouble. It is then that we get hurt and things start going wrong for us. On this earth there are many people that do the devil's will. Jesus teaches us to pray that God's will be done on earth. We must choose to do God's will, so that the earth can become a better place. I know I want to choose God.

What about you? Let's pray that God's will be done in our homes and in our city.

BREAD FOR EACH DAY

"Give us today the food we need."
(Matthew 6:11, NLT)

We all need food, like bread, to stay alive. Your mom and dad probably work every day for money to buy food. There are, however, many poor people in countries all over the world. They are terribly hungry all the time, and they don't even know if they will live until the next day. We must pray for them and help them in whatever way we can.

Because God is our Father, we trust Him to take care of us. The Lord promises in His Word that He will not allow His children to go hungry. He will look after us if we really follow Him and make Him the King of our lives.

Let's thank Him for everything He gives us, and let's give hungry people around us some of His bread.

HE FORGIVES ME

" ... and forgive us our sins."
(Matthew 6:12, NLT)

Jesus came to live on earth and to die on a cross so that God would forgive our sins. All of us are sinful. We are born with sin. Even when we are little, we do things that are wrong, and that is why we all need to be forgiven.

If our sins are not forgiven, we have not made our peace with God. That is why God wants our sins to be forgiven. Actually, He is just waiting for us to say that we are sorry, and then He forgives us immediately. We must never be too proud or unwilling to tell God that we are sorry about our sins.

That is why Jesus taught us to pray, "Forgive us our sins."

I FORGIVE YOU

" ... as we have forgiven those who sin against us." (Matthew 6:12, NLT)

Sometimes we find it difficult to forgive others. But if God forgives us so quickly, then we can also forgive a friend that has hurt us.

If a friend says, "I'm sorry," tell him or her right away, "I forgive you." Even if they don't apologize, forgive them in your heart. When you forgive someone, there is peace in your heart and your life is clean before God. It is the same when God forgives you.

When you have done something that hurt your friend, you must be prepared to say, "Please forgive me. I'm sorry I did this to you." If your friend forgives you then everything is forgotten. If your friend does not want to forgive you, you know that you have done the right thing and that God is proud of you. Be a peacemaker for Christ.

THE SPIDER'S WEB

"And don't let us yield to temptation ... "
(Matthew 6:13, NLT)

A spider spins a web to catch insects to eat. The web may look nice, but if an insect flies into it, it's finished.

Jesus taught us to pray that we would not give in to temptation. That means not getting involved in things that can trap us like insects in a spider's web. The devil also spins a web for us. It looks very inviting, but once we are in his power, he destroys our lives.

When we do something we must always ask God if it is His will for us. Sometimes we are tempted to take someone else's things, or to tell a lie, or to talk behind someone's back. It is not good to do that.

Let's ask God to help us so that we can tell when we are being tempted and to be strong enough to say no to the devil.

THE NASTY OLD SPIDER

" ... but rescue us from the evil one."
(Matthew 6:13, NLT)

Like a spider spins a web to catch insects so that it can kill them, so the devil wants to catch us. The devil is the one who fights against God and His children and wants to destroy us.

Jesus taught us to pray that we may be rescued from the evil one. There is only one way that we can be saved, and that is when the Great Savior, Jesus, protects us. The devil wanted Jesus dead, but Jesus is much stronger than the devil. Jesus rose from the dead and in this way, He defeated the devil.

We must also take sides with Jesus against the devil so that he cannot catch us. We do not belong to the devil, we belong to Jesus. Say no to the devil and yes to Jesus today.

SAYING AMEN

"Father ... not my will, but Yours be done."
(Luke 22:42)

Our prayers usually end with the word Amen. This means "let it be so." It is almost like wishing that what I have just prayed will come true.

But we can only say "Amen" if that which we have prayed is God's will. Many times we think we know what is good for us, but God knows better. I have asked Him for so many things that I did not get, and later on I saw that it was better that way. All the time God knew best. We can really trust Him with our prayers.

By all means, pour your heart out to God. It's all right to tell Him what you would like to have. But then, make sure in your heart that what you are asking for is His will for you. Then you can safely end your prayer with "Amen."

TAKE HIS HAND

"No one can snatch them out of My Father's hand." (John 10:29)

A child knows he is safe when his father takes his hand, especially if he has to cross a busy road or walk in the dark. God asks us to put our hands in His big, strong hand.

We don't always know what tomorrow will bring. We need help. Apart from that, we often do not know what road to take. That is why a Christian puts his or her hand in the big, strong hand of the Father. He will show us the right way. He will not let go of us. He will keep us safe. The Bible says if we put our hand in His, no one can snatch us out of His hand.

Put your hand in His hand right now. Ask Him to lead you through this day. He will hold you tight.

IT HURTS

I consider that our present sufferings are not worth comparing with the glory that will be revealed in us. (Romans 8:18)

At some time or another, you have been hurt. Perhaps you are sick. Because we are not in heaven yet, we will suffer pain.

Jesus knew pain and suffering. He was hurt very badly when He was nailed to the cross for us. But one day all the hurt in our lives will be over. There is no pain and suffering in heaven. This is because Jesus paid for our sins. Because of His pain and suffering, a day will come when we will not hurt in any way anymore.

Perhaps you are hurting now – in your body or your heart. Give the hurt to Jesus. Ask Him to comfort you. He knows pain, and He understands how you feel.

SPEAK GOOD WORDS

The tongue of the wise brings healing.
(Proverbs 12:18)

Isn't it wonderful that we can talk to each other and understand each other? Words can heal or hurt. Words are very powerful.

The Bible says that the tongue is important because it can have a great influence on people. If you encourage someone with your words, it can mean a great deal to that person. But with your words you can also criticize people and hurt them.

The Bible says our tongues must be under God's control. We must ask God to keep our tongues in check so that we don't hurt others. You get a nice feeling in your heart when you speak good words. Good, positive, uplifting words mean a lot to others. I hope you remember that when you speak to your friends.

Ask God to help you speak only good, pleasant words to people today.

THE SULKY MINISTER

This change of plans greatly upset Jonah, and he became very angry. (Jonah 4:1, NLT)

God sent Jonah to a big city called Nineveh. But Jonah didn't want to go. He tried to run away from God and boarded a ship to Tarshish, which was going in the opposite direction.

God told a fish to swallow Jonah. Then Jonah changed his mind and went to Nineveh. But when Jonah saw that God was not going to punish the people there, he became very angry. He went and sat outside the city, sulking.

Instead of being thankful that God was kind to the people of Nineveh, Jonah wanted God to punish them. And all because Jonah didn't like them!

We must not be like Jonah. We must be happy when God's love changes people's lives, and we must also be willing to go if God sends us to talk to someone.

YOU MUST CHOOSE

"Choose today whom you will serve. But as for me and my family, we will serve the LORD." (Joshua 24:15, NLT)

The Bible says we must choose whom we want to serve. Some people don't want anything to do with God, don't believe He exists, or they are afraid of Him.

You and I choose the Lord because we know He is the true God and because it is worth our while to serve Him. We choose God by saying yes to Him: "Yes, Lord, here is my life, here is my heart, here is my everything. I want to follow You and I want to live for You." This is what Joshua and his family did. They decided to listen to God and do what He said.

Have you made your choice for God yet? Do it now and tell Him that you want to serve Him.

THE REAL GOD

For there is one God. (1 Timothy 2:5)

There are many religions in the world. Every religion has its own so-called god. Some people worship Hindu gods, some follow the Buddha, some pray to their ancestors, and some worship the devil.

The Bible tells us very clearly that there is only one real God. His name is God Almighty, the Father of Jesus Christ. All the other gods will bow down before Him one day. If we worship this God, we are safe and we are fortunate. He is a God of love. He loved us so much that He sent His Son so that we could be washed clean from sin.

Across the world there are many people who worship other gods. We must make it very clear that the only real God is the father of Jesus. He is our God and our heavenly Father.

CONTROL YOURSELF

The fruit of the Spirit is self-control.
(Galatians 5:22, 23)

To control a horse most people put a metal bit into its mouth. Without the bit and bridle, the horse would just run where it wants. In the same way, a powerful truck has brakes. Brakes slow it down so that it does not get out of control and cause an accident.

People also need to be controlled. Some people break things or hurt others in a fit of temper. Others take things that don't belong to them.

The One that can really help us is the Holy Spirit. When He is in our lives, He helps us to control our behavior. This means that we won't fly off the handle. He helps us make the right decisions.

Open up your heart to the Holy Spirit. Ask Him to fill you so that you can be under His control.

STICK TO THE RULES

Everyone must submit himself to the governing authorities. (Romans 13:1)

When you play sports you have to play by the rules of the game. If you don't, the referee will blow the whistle. It is important to have rules, otherwise everyone would do just as they please.

Schools and countries also have rules like the speed limit or not stealing. If you don't obey them, you are in trouble. You can be found guilty and must pay a fine, or even worse, go to jail.

Christians try to glorify God in everything they do. And the Lord tells us to obey the rules of a country. God likes to have order, and He likes us to do things the right way. Let's keep the rules of our country and obey what they tell us so that we can please God.

See that you stick to the rules today.

FLAT OUT FOR JESUS

Do you not know that in a race all the runners run, but only one gets the prize? Run in such a way as to get the prize.
(1 Corinthians 9:24)

Athletes taking part in a race give their best. They run flat out because they hope to win.

The Bible says it is almost as if every person on earth is running a race of life. There is a finish line and a prize. But the prize at the end of our lives is not just for winners, but for everyone who believes in Jesus. The Bible says that the one who doesn't give up will win the prize.

This means that we must keep believing in and living for God, even if we are having a hard time. Read your Bible and talk to Him. This will help you not to get spiritually tired. Give your everything today to follow in Jesus' steps.

WASHING FEET

After that, He poured water into a basin and began to wash the disciples' feet.
(John 13:5, NLT)

In Jesus' time, most people walked on foot from one place to another. The streets were dusty and sandy, so their feet got very dirty. When they reached their destination, someone usually brought them water to wash their feet. Sometimes a servant washed their feet.

Jesus didn't think He was too important to wash His disciples' feet. He is our example. Today we don't need to wash a person's feet, but we can follow Jesus' example and treat people well. We can make them feel at home when they visit us. We can be friendly and listen to them. We can give them food or money or love, and we can pay attention to them.

Think of ways how you can "wash someone's feet" today.

HE IS CALLING YOU

Then the LORD called Samuel. Samuel answered, "Here I am." (1 Samuel 3:4)

In the Garden of Eden, Adam and Eve were with God. God talked to them every day, and they always knew He was there. But then they sinned and had to leave paradise. They hid from God, and the Bible says that He called them. Ever since that time God calls people to come to Him. We read in the Old Testament that God called Isaiah and Jeremiah.

Samuel was just a little boy when God called him. The Lord wanted Samuel to follow Him. When Samuel heard the Lord calling him, he answered, "Speak, Lord, for Your servant is listening."

Even today the Lord calls people to come to Him. He wants to forgive their sins and use them. He also calls you. And He calls me. I have answered yes. Have you said yes to Him yet? Do it now.

HE KNOWS EVERYTHING

Everything is naked and exposed before His eyes, and He is the one to whom we are accountable. (Hebrews 4:13, NLT)

Have you ever done something that you kept quiet about? You thought nobody would ever find out. Sometimes we manage to hide things from people. But we can't hide anything from God. He knows everything that happens on earth. He knows everything we do and think. That is why it is impossible to hide anything from Him. The sooner we realize that, the sooner we can be honest about our sins.

Fortunately, God is a God of love. He wants to forgive us. When we have done something wrong, all we have to do is tell Him we're sorry.

If we do not confess our sins, we will have to account for them one day before the throne of God. It is better to say you're sorry now. He will forgive you right away.

THE SAVIOR OF THE WORLD

"We know that this man really is the Savior of the world." (John 4:42)

Have you and your friends ever played a game where you tie up someone? When somebody's hands and feet are tied up, he or she can hardly move. They can't untie themselves. They need someone else to free or save them.

The Bible says Jesus is called the Savior. He came to save us from sin, hell and the devil. The name "Jesus" comes from the word Yeshua, which means "to loose or loosen." Jesus was sent to untie the shackles and cords of the devil. Only He can free us.

So many people are still bound tightly by their sins. We must tell them that Jesus is the Savior. I hope you have already asked the Lord to free you from sin and save you.

NOT RULES, LOVE

Love does no harm to its neighbor. Therefore love is the fulfillment of the law.
(Romans 13:10)

Some people think that to follow God means to keep a lot of rules, and the moment they break some rule, they are in trouble. But God is not like that at all.

In the Old Testament, the children of God had to obey certain rules and laws. But they couldn't, because they were sinners. That's why God sent Jesus. Jesus proved His love for us when He died for us to pay for our sins. Now we are so thankful that we want to show Jesus how much we love Him, and that is why we do what He wants. We want to make Him happy.

We needn't worry about a lot of rules, but we must do what He would like us to do because we love Him.

I AM AFRAID

In God I trust; I will not be afraid.
(Psalm 56:11)

Maybe you are afraid that something unpleasant or terrible will happen to you today. Maybe you didn't study for a test. Perhaps you are afraid of other things, like death. Everybody is afraid at some time or another.

When we are afraid, we must give our fear to God. This is what the writer of this psalm did. He called on the name of the Lord. Another psalm says the name of the Lord is like a strong tower, and if we go in there, we will be safe. Give your fear to God today. Tell Him what scares you. Ask Him to help you. I am sure He will, because He promises to do just that in His Word.

The Lord wants us to trust Him. We must thank Him and praise Him for that.

I AM SENDING YOU

"Therefore go and make disciples of all nations." (Matthew 28:19)

God decided to do His work here on earth using not only angels (that we can't see), but especially human beings. He uses people like you and me – not just the pastor or some or other important person in the church.

We read in the Bible that God called many people to do His work. He called Moses to lead His people. He called Gideon to fight against the enemy. He called Samuel to serve Him in the temple. He called Esther to save the people of Israel. He called Mary to raise Jesus. God also calls us because He has work to do and He wants us to help Him.

God is calling you today. Go to the nations, or simply go to your classmates or your friends. You just have to be willing. Tell Him, "Yes, Lord, I am ready. Use me."

JUST LIKE AN EAGLE

Like an eagle that stirs up its nest and hovers over its young, that spreads its wings to catch them (Deuteronomy 32:11, 12)

Eagles are beautiful birds. They live high up in the mountains on rock ledges.

There they build their nests and hatch their eggs. But one day the mother eagle throws the baby out of the nest so that it falls down the steep cliff. The next moment the mother eagle spreads her wings, catches the baby and takes it back to the nest. The next moment she does everything all over again. The baby falls, flaps its wings, and she catches it. This is the way it learns to fly.

God does the same to us. All the difficult times in our lives teach us to fly and to grow spiritually strong. Thank God for the difficult times in your life. These will make you spiritually mighty.

BITTER FRUIT

See to it that no bitter root grows up to cause trouble. (Hebrews 12:15)

Some fruit trees give us the most tasty fruit. But there are also trees that give us bitter fruit. This fruit is not nice to eat.

The Bible says we are like a tree. We can bear good or bad fruit. We bear sweet fruit when we behave according to God's will. But bitterness makes our fruit taste really bad.

Bitterness is when you are cross with someone and you are not prepared to forgive them. Then there is bitterness in your heart toward them, which affects your whole life. You become a grumpy, sour person, and others don't like being with you.

Are you perhaps not prepared to forgive someone today? Are you bitter? Tell God now that you forgive that person, and your bitterness will go away.

A LITTLE BECOMES A LOT

After everyone was full ... they picked up the pieces and filled twelve baskets with scraps left by the people who had eaten. (John 6:12-13, NLT)

When Jesus was on earth, one of the miracles He performed was increasing a little boy's fish and bread.

There were thousands of people who became very hungry as they sat listening to Jesus. When He asked if anyone had food, a little boy brought Him two small fish and five loaves of bread. Jesus took the food and broke it, and the disciples handed it out. In front of their eyes, it became more and there were even leftovers!

I think Jesus wanted to show that even the little that we give Him can become a lot in His hands. Don't you want to give what you have today – your talents, beauty, sport, whatever – to Jesus? He will use it and many people will be blessed by it.

WONDERFUL COUNSELOR

He will be called Wonderful Counselor.
(Isaiah 9:6)

The Holy Spirit prophesied that Jesus would be born for us and that His name would be "Wonderful." That means that no one is as fantastic as Jesus.

Everybody on earth has faults, and therefore we must forgive others. Sometimes we have to be patient with people. It's no fun having to deal with the weaknesses of others all the time. But Jesus had no faults, and He never sinned. It must have been wonderful to be with Him.

Because Jesus is so wonderful, we praise and glorify Him and tell others that it is worthwhile following Him. Praise Him because you know He is wonderful and because you love Him. The greatest miracle is that He loves us so much that He died on a cross for us.

THE ROARING LION

Stay alert! Watch out for your great enemy, the devil. He prowls around like a roaring lion. (1 Peter 5:8, NLT)

The Bible tells us that the devil is just like a roaring lion. He wants to devour and destroy us. Many people's lives have been destroyed because they listened to the devil. Many things we see on TV or read about seem so exciting. But everything that is not the Lord's will – no matter how much fun it seems to be – is not good for us. We must trust that God always knows what's best for us.

The best way to avoid the devil is to follow God. Tell Jesus, now, that you love Him and that you want to do what He says. Read the Bible and talk to God every day. That will upset the devil.

Choose God today.

PEACE FOR THE WORLD

" ... and on earth peace to those on whom His favor rests." (Luke 2:14)

There is a lot of fighting all over the world. Between families, friends, countries, and nations.

When Jesus was born, the angels sang that there was a chance for peace on earth. Another name for Jesus is "Prince of Peace." Jesus wants so badly for us to have peace in our hearts. That is why He offers us peace when He forgives our sins. When our sins have been taken away by Jesus, we also find peace with God the Father.

After that you must still make peace with your fellow humans. We sometimes have arguments, but we want to say we're sorry afterward and make peace.

Are you in conflict with someone today? Make peace. Be God's instrument of peace in your class, your school, your home, your town, and even the whole world.

PAID FOR AND ERASED

He took it away, nailing it to the cross.
(Colossians 2:14)

It feels good to erase a mistake you have made in your schoolwork. With an eraser, correction fluid, or the delete button you can remove all mistakes easily and start again.

We all make mistakes, but mistakes can be corrected. The greatest problem in a person's life is sin. Sin makes us miss God's purpose in our lives and do the wrong thing. How can we be washed clean from sin? The Bible has good news: there is Someone who can erase our sins. His name is Jesus Christ.

When Jesus died on the cross, He paid for our sins with His blood. His death on the cross can erase our sins.

Give your life to the Lord today and ask Him to erase all your sins. Then you can stand before Him, clean.

HALLELUJAH

Give thanks to the LORD, for He is good.
(Psalm 118:1)

One of the best words in the Bible is hallelujah. In some modern translations of the Bible the words "praise the Lord" are used instead of "hallelujah."

To me "praise the Lord" sounds more like an order than a suggestion. It's almost as if the Bible tells us that we must praise the Lord. Naturally! After all, He is the Great King of heaven and earth. There is nobody like Him. Of course we must tell everybody that He is great and wonderful.

We praise the Lord when we say that He is great and good. We can also sing this with all our heart. The original meaning of the word "hallelujah" is actually to be proud of the Lord.

Are you proud of the Lord? Then tell others that He is great and wonderful.

BEING THANKFUL

... being watchful and thankful.
(Colossians 4:2)

Some people complain about things all the time, as if nothing is ever good enough for them. Being unthankful is a very ugly characteristic. If you sit down and think, you will find many things to be thankful for. Think of the beauty of nature, friendly people, nourishing food, a home, a warm bed, a car to take us places.

But the best thing of all is that Jesus came and changed our lives with His love. When a heart is filled with His love, it overflows with thankfulness and spills over onto others. Then we can find something to be thankful for even in the most difficult circumstances. Start right now and get into the habit of looking on the bright side and say "thank you" for it. The Bible says we must be thankful for everything. What can you thank God for today?

LIKE FATHER, LIKE SON

... until Christ is formed in you.
(Galatians 4:19)

You have probably heard the expression, "Like father, like son" or, "Like mother, like daughter." It means that someone acts just like their mom or dad or looks like one of them.

God wants us to look like Him. When He becomes our heavenly Father, when we understand what He wants from us and we hear Him talk to us, then we will begin to think and act like Him more and more. Paul wrote a letter to Christians and encouraged them to look more and more like Jesus. By acting and thinking like Jesus, people will know they belong to Him.

Ask the Lord to help you become more and more like Him. When people see how you live and hear what you say, they should know you are a Christian.

BLESS YOUR ENEMY

Bless those who persecute you; bless and do not curse. (Romans 12:14)

Enemies are people who do not like one another one bit. Perhaps there is someone that you don't like very much.

Although we don't have to like everybody, it doesn't mean they must be our enemies. Maybe there's a bully in your school who makes you unhappy and feels like an enemy. Christians should not respond as others would.

The Bible says we must bless our enemies. You must say, "I want the best for you in life. May God pour His love out over you." But you must also say, "May God work in your life so that you are also filled with love and goodness." Someone who comes closer to Jesus will have a change of heart. Then he or she doesn't want to be an enemy anymore, but a friend. Ask God now to bless your "enemy".

HOW GREAT ARE YOU?

"Whoever wants to become great among you must be your servant." (Mark 10:43)

We all know important people like sports stars or actors. They are great in the eyes of people because they have achieved success.

Jesus said clearly that if you want to be great or important, you must be prepared to serve others. This means that greatness is not about being famous, but about helping and supporting others by loving and serving them. Leaders who always want their own way, and who push others around as it suits them are not great in God's eyes. A true leader is someone who works hard, supports others, and wants to help.

How can you serve someone today? What can you do to help others? Perhaps a friend needs your help. Go and serve him or her. Then you will be great in the eyes of the Lord, and people will respect you.

THE HUMBLE

"God opposes the proud but gives grace to the humble." (James 4:6, NLT)

Arrogant people are a real pain! Their attitude says, "I am better than you." They think they are very important and want everybody to think so too. God does not like this kind of pride, because it causes you to look down on others and treat them disrespectfully. Proud people should realize that they are small in God's eyes, and they should treat others with respect.

A humble person admits their own shortcomings and faults. They accept their talents and good qualities, but don't think they are better than others. They also thank God for everything they have received. God will give such people grace.

Thank God that you are who you are, but also tell Him you know you have faults and that you need Him. Ask Him to help you build others up and enrich them.

DRINKING FROM A DIRTY CUP

*If you keep yourself pure, you will be a
special utensil for honorable use.
(2 Timothy 2:21)*

There are utensils for everyday use, but there are also things for special occasions. Mom doesn't use her best cups every day, but when important guests visit, she brings out her best china. When we work in the garden, we wear just any old thing. Our best clothes we keep for special occasions.

The Bible says that we must be instruments for a specific purpose: "some utensils are made of gold and silver, and some are made of wood and clay. The expensive utensils are used for special occasions, and the cheap ones are for everyday use" (2 Timothy 2:20). We can be very special instruments for God if we keep ourselves pure. To do this, we must confess our sins and obey God. Ask Him to wash you clean of sin and do His will.

BELIEVE AND DO

What good is it if a man claims to have faith but has no deeds? (James 2:14)

Many people say they believe in God. They go to church regularly and do all kinds of nice religious things, but you sometimes wonder if their faith is genuine. The Bible says quite clearly if we say we believe, then our deeds must show our faith.

This means that it is not enough to read the Bible and know it well; we must apply it to our lives. For example, we should not steal or swear, and we should forgive others. To follow Jesus is to believe in Him and to do what He says. Faith without deeds means nothing.

Let's try to follow God properly. Let's ask Him to help us today not only to believe in Him, but also to do what He says.

DON'T KICK ME

If someone is caught in a sin, you ... should restore him gently. (Galatians 6:1)

If someone shows weakness, it's easy to point a finger at them, judge them or gossip about it. In this way, the people pointing the finger often feel good about themselves.

I'm sure you've heard the saying, "Don't kick a man when he's down." What we are really saying is, "Why keep on criticizing someone who has made a mistake?" Forget it so that they can put it behind them. As Paul says in 1 Corinthians 13:5, "Love ... keeps no record of wrongs."

The Bible admits that people sometimes sin, but it says that we must not keep criticizing them for it. Rather, we should be gentle and help them. We must be prepared to forgive, to be friendly, to help them work things out.

Don't take pleasure in someone's wrongs today – help them.

REST WELL

He said to them, "Come with Me to a quiet place and get some rest." (Mark 6:31)

Holidays are fun because we can relax at home, or visit friends, or go away to a holiday resort. Holidays are necessary so that we can rest.

Everyone needs time to rest. Even Jesus realized that He and His disciples had to rest, and that is why He called them to one side and said, "Let's just get away from the crowds for a while to get some rest and relax in a peaceful, quiet place."

I hope you will take time to enjoy holidays or school breaks when you have them. See to it, however, that you also make time for God, read your Bible every day, and take Him with you wherever you go. Be His witness. Tell people about Him.

Fill your days with Jesus, and you will go back to school refreshed.

SAMSON'S MISTAKE

Samson fell in love with a woman in the Valley of Sorek whose name was Delilah. (Judges 16:4)

God gave Samson great strength because He had a plan for him.

The Israelites believed in God, and were forbidden to marry someone outside their nation, because other people didn't believe in the Lord.

Samson fell in love with Delilah, a Philistine woman who didn't believe in God. Against God's will, Samson decided to marry Delilah. If we don't do what God wants, we are looking for trouble. In the end, Delilah cut Samson's hair, his strength left him, and he was overcome by the Philistines. Soon afterward he died.

It is not too soon for you to start praying that God will help you marry the right person someday. Don't do what Samson did; ask for God's will.

TOO YOUNG

"Ah, Sovereign LORD, I am only a child."
(Jeremiah 1:6)

It's wonderful that God uses people like us to do His work. He has a place and a task for each of us. Nobody is unimportant in His eyes.

Jeremiah was young when God called him. He had to go and talk to the people of Israel about their sins and to bring them to God. Jeremiah's first reaction was that he was far too young. They would not listen to him. But God wanted to use him and no one else.

God does not just use older people He also calls children. There may just be something He wants you to do. Because Jeremiah was prepared to be used by God, He worked for the Lord for about fifty years as a minister. I don't know what God's plan is with you; just tell Him that you will be willing when He calls you.

GOD'S PLAN

She got a papyrus basket. Then she placed the child in it and put it among the reeds along the bank of the Nile. (Exodus 2:3)

At the time Moses was born, the pharaoh was worried about the many Israelites in Egypt. He ordered that all the baby Israelite boys be killed.

Moses' mother loved him very much, so she put him in a basket and hid him on the bank of the Nile river.

But God always has a plan for our lives. He wanted to use Moses to lead the Israelites out of Egypt. God saw to it that the pharaoh's daughter found Moses. He grew up in the palace and became a leader. When he was older, God told him to take the Israelites out of Egypt.

God has a plan for each of us. Follow Him and trust Him. Do what He asks you to. He can use you.

WHAT A SURPRISE!

At this, she turned around and saw Jesus standing there. (John 20:14)

Mary Magdalene was once surprised by Jesus. She had been a very bad woman before she met Him. He taught her about peace and forgiveness and told her about His kingdom.

She believed Him and it changed her life. She started loving Jesus as her Savior.

Then Jesus died on the cross. Mary's heart was broken. She must have cried a lot. Three days after Jesus' death she went to His grave. There a wonderful surprise waited for her. She saw Jesus standing there, alive! She couldn't believe her eyes. This was the greatest surprise of her life. He was alive!

If we give our lives to Jesus, we find that He is just as wonderful toward us as He was to Mary. And He is alive in our hearts.

TREASURE IN YOUR HEART

"For where your treasure is, there your heart will be also." (Luke 12:34)

When you have been given something precious, you want to keep it close to you. If you have a shiny new bicycle, you won't leave it at school overnight. You want it near you because you are so happy about it. And you want to look after it, "treasure it". In the same way, when you love someone, you want to be with that person.

The Bible tells us to keep the right treasures in our hearts: the things of the Lord's kingdom. God and our relationship with Him are much more important than bicycles, cars, video games, clothes, or money. Of course it's nice to have these things, but they are not more important than our relationship with God.

Make sure that Jesus is most important in your life.

RESIST THE DEVIL

Resist the devil, and he will flee from you.
(James 4:7)

The devil comes with all kinds of lies and tries to lure you away from God. To know when it is the devil talking to us, we need to know the Bible. The Bible tells us what God's will is. When thoughts come into our minds, and they are not from the Bible, we can know they are from the devil. Then we need to tell ourselves loud and clear not to be disobedient to God. In this way we resist the devil, and he has no power over us.

We can never resist the devil in our own strength. But if we resist him in the name of God, we will win. Is there something in your life that you know is not God's will? Decide now to do God's will and resist the devil, then he can do nothing to you.

BE HONEST

He who conceals his sins does not prosper,
but whoever confesses and renounces them
finds mercy. (Proverbs 28:13)

Wanting to hide failure and sin is natural to all of humankind. If you spill something on your mom's new tablecloth, you quickly put a plate on the stain so that no one will notice it.

When we sin, it always makes us feel a bit afraid and we want to hide. But the Bible says if we hide our sin, we cannot be forgiven. We need to be honest about our sins and tell God everything. Tell Him you are sorry; He will forgive you. You must also tell people you are sorry if you have treated them badly.

Do not hide your sins. Apologize and let it go, and God will give you His grace. Grace means the Lord will forgive you and put His loving arms around you.

WHAT IS COOL?

I consider everything a loss compared to the surpassing greatness of knowing Christ.
(Philippians 3:8)

A thing is "cool" when we like it a lot. Then we tell all our friends about it. This is what Paul did.

Paul was on the road one day when a bright light fell on him. It was Jesus, who had a special plan for him. This changed his whole life. He got to know God, and from that day on, everything he thought was cool before, was not cool anymore.

Paul writes that the coolest thing on earth is to know the Lord, to love Him, and to follow Him.

God wants you to be excited about things that make you happy. Just make sure that He is not pushed to one side. I pray that the coolest thing on earth for you, as it was with Paul, will be to know and serve the Lord.

THROW IT AWAY

Cast all your anxiety on Him because He cares for you. (1 Peter 5:7)

Problems are like a weight on our shoulders. They make us unhappy. And we worry. If you are a Christian, it is wonderful to know that God knows about your problems. The Bible tells us to "cast all your anxiety ... " This means you should throw away the thing that is making your heart heavy. Throw it into the hands of Jesus. Let Him handle it.

How do you do this? In the first place, you must realize that you are worried about something. Ask yourself, "Why am I so worried?" When you have found the answer, tell God about it. Pass it into His hands.

Do it now. Throw away your problems. Give them to Jesus. I am sure He will help.

FACING THE GIANT

A champion named Goliath was over nine feet tall. (1 Samuel 17:4)

Goliath was an enormous Philistine warrior. All the Israelite soldiers were afraid of him and didn't want to fight against him.

Only David was not scared. He had brought his brothers food so that they could be strong for the battle. He saw the giant challenging the Israelites. God then gave David courage. He was only a young boy, but he knew God was greater than Goliath, and he was not afraid. He said to Goliath, "You come against me with sword and spear and javelin, but I come against you in the name of the Lord Almighty."

God was happy about David's faith. So He helped David to defeat the giant.

Even if you are still young, you can, like David, believe in God's great power and the Lord will be able to use you to win a victory.

THE KING'S SIN

Then David said to Nathan, "I have sinned against the LORD." (2 Samuel 12:13)

David was the most important king Israel ever had. He was a good ruler, a brave soldier and he loved God. Many of the psalms in the Bible are songs he sang to God.

Then David made a big mistake. He saw another man's wife and wished that she could be his wife. So, he took her. This was a sin in God's eyes, so He sent a prophet to tell David that it was wrong. David was sorry and confessed his sin to God. He realized it was stealing and it was wrong to use his position as king to do it.

Have you ever taken something that wasn't yours because you wanted it so badly? I hope you told the Lord that you are sorry. God will forgive you if you are sorry about your sins.

RESPECT PEOPLE'S RIGHTS

The law has become paralyzed, and there is no justice in the courts. (Habakkuk 1:4, NLT)

In the book of Habakkuk, the writer asks God why so much is wrong in the world. He sees people fighting and arguing, and the laws of the country have no power anymore. Human rights are violated because bad people have gained the upper hand over good ones.

We could almost believe that Habakkuk is living in our time. All over the world there is fighting. People are oppressed and hurt, and their property is stolen.

This situation makes God sad. We must treat everybody with respect because that is what God wants us to do. If we really love others as God tells us to, then we will not oppress them or hurt them. We will do right by them.

Make an effort today to treat all people with respect.

THE SECRET IS OUT

The mystery that has been kept hidden for ages and generations, but is now disclosed. (Colossians 1:26)

When somebody tells others a secret, then it is not a secret anymore. The wonderful message of Jesus was like a secret to some.

No one in the Old Testament knew who Jesus was. The people of Israel talked about the Messiah that would come, but they didn't quite know who He was and what He would look like.

When Jesus was on earth, He wanted to tell everybody that He came as Savior. He told the disciples to tell everybody that only He is the Way and the Truth and the Life. We know that Jesus is the Savior. This message must be told to everyone. There are still many people all over the world who have never heard of Jesus. To them it is still a secret. Let us tell everybody that Jesus is alive.

A REAL PIG

Therefore, get rid of all moral filth.
(James 1:21)

"You're as dirty as a pig!" This is what we say when someone is very dirty. A pig loves rolling around in the mud and being dirty.

The Bible says sin is dirty. If you have not been washed clean of sin by Jesus, you are just as dirty as that pig rolling in the mud. Only Jesus' sacrifice on the cross can wash you and me clean. I hope you have already asked the Lord to wash your dirty sins clean.

Because we are Christians it will bother us if we keep on sinning. Rather than pigs, we become more like cats that cannot stand getting their feet dirty. If we have sinned, we must want to be washed clean as soon as possible. We tell God we are sorry, and He forgives us.

THE SWEET BOOK

So I ate it, and it tasted as sweet as honey in my mouth. (Ezekiel 3:3)

Honey is very sweet. You can spread it on bread or sweeten your tea or coffee with it.

The Bible uses an image to tell us how good it is when you read the Word of God. Ezekiel saw God coming to him with a scroll on which His words were written. God told Ezekiel to eat this scroll, the Word of God. Ezekiel found that it was as sweet as honey. This explains that the Word of God is always good for us; as healthy as honey.

If we love God, we want to listen to His words. Reading the Bible is just as good for us as eating honey. It gives us more energy and is even tastier. So, you must make sure that you "eat" the Word of God every day.

BRINGING BLESSINGS

The LORD blessed the household of the Egyptian because of Joseph. (Genesis 39:5)

God had a plan for Joseph's life. He allowed Joseph to be taken to a faraway country and sold into slavery. But God looked after Joseph and saw to it that he was taken into service in the house of an important officer named Potiphar.

Because the Lord blessed Joseph, He also blessed the house of Potiphar. This is because Joseph brought the Lord with him to that house.

When you and I serve God, we are His blessed children. Then the Lord walks with us. Wherever we go, He goes with us. In this way we can be a blessing for others wherever we are.

Be a blessing today to your class, or in your church, or among your friends, or on the sports field.

JESUS FORGIVES

Peter left the courtyard, weeping bitterly.
(Luke 22:62, NLT)

When Jesus was captured, His disciples were frightened and ran away. Peter followed Jesus and the soldiers at a distance. When he waited in a courtyard to see what would happen, three people recognized him as one of the disciples. But Peter denied that he had anything to do with Jesus because he was scared of what might happen to him.

Jesus knew beforehand that Peter would do this. He said a rooster would crow to remind Peter that he had let Jesus down. It happened just like that. Peter left and started crying. He was so sorry that he had turned his back on Jesus.

Jesus loved Peter very much, and after He rose from the dead, He forgave Peter. He wants to use us in spite of our weaknesses.

WHY WORRY?

"Therefore do not worry about tomorrow."
(Matthew 6:34)

When we are worried about tomorrow, we don't look forward to it, and we are a bit sad when the new day comes. When you feel like this, you struggle to even smile.

But if you belong to the Lord, you can learn to leave your worries in His hands. You can be cheerful about what waits for you tomorrow and have joy in your heart.

A cheerful, laughing person can better handle all the problems of today and tomorrow. Give your worries to the Lord right now and be thankful that He is in control of your life. Then you will laugh at tomorrow.

This is a good laugh, because you know the Lord will be with you.

WONDERFUL THINGS

LORD, how majestic is Your name in all the earth! (Psalm 8:9)

Even if many things are wrong on earth, like pollution and endangered species, it is still a wonderful place. God made everything very good and beautiful like different kinds of animals, and many kinds of plants in gardens all over the world. Just think of the variety of fish in the sea or the different kinds of birds there are.

God made the earth wonderful. The Bible also says we are crowned with glory and honor (Psalm 8:6). Of everything the Lord made, we are the best. Just think of all the millions of people ... and every one is different. God also gave us minds so that we can rule over the whole world.

Praise and glorify God today for His wonderful creation. Praise Him also for yourself. Let's tell everybody that the Lord's works are wonderful!

ASK, SEEK AND FIND

"Ask, and it will be given to you; seek and you will find; knock and the door will be opened to you." (Luke 11:9)

We all want answers to our questions – we want to find what we are looking for and see doors open for us when we knock. Unfortunately, we often ask the wrong person or persons, look in the wrong places, knock at the wrong doors.

Jesus knows our plight and invites us to come to Him. When we talk to Him, we realize there are things that only He can give, like His redemption and peace. Let's ask Him because He gives freely to those who ask.

Jesus invites everyone to knock at His door. He will open for everyone, and He invites us to join Him in a feast. Jesus opens the right doors for us so that we can live meaningful lives. So, knock at His door, and He will welcome you.

A HEAVY OR A LIGHT WEIGHT

Let us throw off everything that hinders.
(Hebrews 12:1)

There are many heavy loads that we can carry along with us. Things like a heavy suitcase, a friend that we carry on our back, or a bag of groceries. Whenever we carry a load, we need strength.

A load can also be a weight that we carry in our spirit, like worries, hurt and sin. God wants us to travel light. He wants us to feel free and not suffer unnecessary hardships. That is why Jesus came to free us from the heavy weight of sin in our hearts. Many people have so many other things that they have to attend to – like money or cars, or clothes or business problems – that they are not free either.

Throw away the unnecessary baggage or load in your heart. Give it to Jesus and see how free you feel.

A GENTLE ANSWER

A gentle answer turns away wrath.
(Proverbs 15:1)

Someone has probably shouted at you before or talked so loudly that it sounded as if that person was angry with you. Perhaps it was your brother that shouted at you because he was angry with you. The first thing we want to do is shout back. But it is not the best thing to do.

The Bible says it is much better to give a gentle answer. When someone lashes out at you and you are also furious, it can only mean war! It is much better to react to angry words in a soft and gentle manner. This makes the other person cool off.

Let us give a gentle answer when someone has been unkind to us. Let's try it out together. A gentle answer helps so that the devil doesn't win.

WE ALL MAKE MISTAKES

If we claim to be without sin, we deceive ourselves and the truth is not in us.
(1 John 1:8)

Some people pretend to have no faults. They always make excuses, even when they do make a mistake. The Bible says someone like this is misleading or cheating himself. Of course we all have faults! We all sometimes do something wrong.

If we realize that all of us make mistakes, we will be able to forgive more easily. Perhaps we won't be so impatient when someone makes a mistake with us. Because we also make mistakes!

But what should we do when someone has made a mistake? We must start praying for this person right away and forgive him in our hearts. We must say, "I forgive you." And if we have made a mistake, we must say as quickly as possible, "I am sorry! Please forgive me."

EYES ON GOD

We keep looking to the LORD our God for His mercy, just as servants keep their eyes on their master. (Psalm 123:2, NLT)

In the time of the Bible there were many servants. Anytime the master called them they had to be ready. They had to find out what the master wanted and carry out his orders. In exchange for their service, the master took care of them.

Psalm 123 says that in the same way, our eyes must be on the Lord. We must always be ready to serve Him and please Him. What He asks us to do, we must do. We must keep our eyes open and not leave His side. We must be available and notice it immediately when He indicates that we are needed. In this way we are of service to Him and we please Him.

Keep your eyes on the Lord today.

THE VIOLENT WIND

Suddenly a sound like the blowing of a violent wind came from heaven. All of them were filled with the Holy Spirit. (Acts 2:2, 4)

When the wind blows, you hear its sound through the trees, but you cannot see the wind itself.

While the disciples were together, waiting for the Holy Spirit to come, they heard something which sounded like a violent wind blowing. Earthly winds are very strong and can lift the roofs from buildings. Hurricanes have blown whole houses away in coastal areas.

The image of the wind tells us that the Holy Spirit is also very powerful. Just as the wind can blow into a room and blow things over, the Holy Spirit can come into us and change our lives.

Don't be afraid of the Holy Spirit. He will never hurt us. Ask Him to blow into your life and to fill your heart with His power.

THE HELPER

The Spirit helps us in our weakness.
(Romans 8:26)

Another name for the Holy Spirit is the "helper." Sometimes we are really in need of help when we feel weak or are in some kind of trouble.

This is when the Holy Spirit helps. He pleads for us with the Father the moment that He notices we are in trouble, and inside our spirit He gives us hope and strength. The Holy Spirit is a wonderful Person. He is our helper. No matter what difficult situation we get into, He is also in that situation, because He lives in us. If someone tries to hurt us, He feels it too. He shares everything with us, and He is the one who gives us strength when we are weak.

Thank the Holy Spirit, now, that He is also your helper – today and for the rest of your life.

THE ADVOCATE

The Spirit Himself intercedes for us with groans that words cannot express.
(Romans 8:26)

An advocate's job is to defend people's cases in court when they have been charged with a crime. They help prove that you are not guilty, or if you are, help that you perhaps get a lighter sentence.

The devil brings a charge against every one of us. In Revelation 12:10 he is called "the accuser of our brothers." These are the people who believe in God. He enjoys accusing us. He loves telling the Lord that we are not good enough because we have sinned again! He is always busy accusing us.

Fortunately the Holy Spirit is our Advocate. He speaks for us and defends our case. He pleads for us with the Father. He helps us in difficult times. The Holy Spirit is our heavenly Advocate.

MY BEST FRIEND

Jonathan became one in spirit with David,
and he loved him as himself.
(1 Samuel 18:1)

When you have a best friend, you enjoy visiting each other and showing that you love each other.

As a young man, David met Jonathan, King Saul's son. Soon David and Jonathan saw that they liked each other very much, and they became best friends. They could tell each other their deepest secrets. When one was in trouble, the other stood by him.

I hope you have a very special friend. And even more so, I hope you are also a very special friend to someone. To have a best friend, you must also be a good friend. You must accept your friend just the way they are, be loving, and prove to that person that you can be trusted. Ask God to help you be a good friend to someone.

ALL ALONE

"My God, My God, why have You forsaken Me?" (Matthew 27:46)

Sometimes we are alone, and sometimes we feel lonely. Lonely is when you feel like everyone's left you and your heart hurts. This is how Jesus felt when He was hanging on the cross.

Jesus had to go through the worst of the worst for us. For a moment on the cross the Father had to, in a sense, turn His back on His Son. At that moment Jesus knew that He was completely alone. The nails hurt His hands, and the wounds the soldiers gave Him were painful.

When Jesus asked why the Father had forsaken Him, He felt lonely and deserted. If we believe in Him, we need never be lonely any more. Not even on the day that we die. He promised that He will always be with us.

JUST CARRY ON

The men who were guarding Jesus began mocking and beating Him. (Luke 22:63)

While Jesus was on earth, people mocked Him after He was captured. The soldiers hit Him and said ugly things to Him. Even when Jesus was nailed to the cross and suffering, they did not stop.

Because the devil does not like Jesus at all, he will do everything he can to destroy the work and message of Jesus. One of his methods is to get people to make fun of Jesus, His followers and His kingdom. Perhaps there is someone who teases you because you pray, or read your Bible. Don't let it get to you. Carry on. Even if people make fun of you, you know that they will stand before God's throne one day.

In the meantime, pray for those people and love them, just like Jesus did.

GOOD FRIDAY

... carrying His own cross to the place of the skull. Here they crucified Him.
(John 19:17, 18)

Good Friday is the day we remember Jesus' death on the cross at the place of the skull, Golgotha.

Jesus was completely innocent, yet He was captured, beaten and led outside Jerusalem to be executed like a criminal. Jesus was not a criminal; He was innocent when He was nailed to a cross. A crown made of thorns was pushed hard into His head, and He was bleeding. He suffered terribly before He died. Why?

He gave His life so that we wouldn't have to die because of our sins. Tell the Lord Jesus how thankful you are. Decide now to give Him your life as He gave His to you. Praise Him, serve Him, tell others that you have a wonderful Savior. Without Him we would all have died in sin.

SOAP AND BLOOD

The blood of Jesus, His Son, purifies us from all sin. (1 John 1:7)

One day a man explained why he did not believe in Jesus. He said Jesus died on the cross for us two thousand years ago and yet the world had not changed much.

If Jesus had really come to forgive people and to take the sins away, why was there so much sin still in the world? Another man answered that there is soap all over the world but some people are still dirty. This was because they did not take the soap and wash themselves. Soap washes away dirt only if you use it.

It works exactly the same way with the blood of Jesus. Jesus' blood was shed for our sins. Yet there are many people who do not believe and accept this.

Everyone who accepts, in faith, Jesus' death on the cross is washed clean of sin.

ALREADY ROLLED AWAY

They were on their way to the tomb and they asked each other, "Who will roll the stone away from the entrance of the tomb?" (Mark 16:2, 3)

After Jesus' death, the women who knew Him well went to His grave. On their way there, they wondered how they would roll the big stone away from the entrance. In those days people were buried in graves that looked like small rooms.

But an angel had already rolled the stone away because Jesus had risen from the dead.

We are often just like these women. We worry about how something can be done. The task ahead looks impossible. But when we get to the stage where we have to do something about it, we find that Jesus has already seen to it. Ask God, in time, to help you. He will see to it that you will be able to do the work.

GOD IN YOUR HOUSE

He has remembered His faithfulness to the house of Israel. (Psalm 98:3)

Homes are wonderful places with beds, plates, pictures and many other things. But more important in a house than things, are people. There are many houses with a bad atmosphere. There are arguments and unhappiness, but no peace or love. A home like this needs God.

God wants to reconfirm His love and faithfulness to every house in Israel (according to Psalm 98). And to your house as well. If you love God, pray that His love and faithfulness will reign in your house. Pray for your mom and dad and the rest of your family. Pray that the Holy Spirit will be in your house. Pray for love that comes from God. Just keep on praying, even if it doesn't seem to be working.

Keep on praying that the Lord will be King in your house.

LIGHT IN THE DARKNESS

"You are the light of the world."
(Matthew 5:14)

Most towns and cities have streetlights that shine brightly so that people who travel at night can see where they are going. The Bible says it is as if the world is dark with all the sin in people's lives.

It's spiritually dark in the hearts of many people and in their homes. Their lives are without any purpose, empty and without direction. Jesus said He is the light of the world. When you believe in Him, you receive light, so that you can live a meaningful life.

As His children, we must be like a shining light. If He lives in our hearts, we shine brightly in a dark world. I hope you are like a streetlight that shines in your street, your neighborhood, and town.

Let's ask God that His light will burn brightly in us today.

SITTING OR MOVING?

He spoke with great fervor and taught about Jesus accurately. (Acts 18:25)

Some Christians seem to be sitting comfortably in the armchair of their faith. They don't really seem excited and enthusiastic about the things of the Lord.

Enthusiasm means that you are excited and glad about something and want to share it with others. It comes from two Greek words that mean "God is in you." If the Lord really lives in us, we are enthusiastic. About what? About Jesus, of course, and about His kingdom.

I hope you are not someone who does nothing. I hope you want to move about and excitedly talk about Jesus and His kingdom. A Christian like this is on fire in their spirit.

Let's ask the Holy Spirit to fill us with enthusiasm for the God's kingdom.

TAKE OFF THE HANDCUFFS

... to proclaim freedom for the captives.
(Isaiah 61:1)

Isaiah prophesied many years ago that Jesus would come to do important work.

The Spirit of God would equip Him for the task and anoint Him. He would become the Savior of the world. He would proclaim freedom for everyone in captivity. This is an image the Bible uses to say that anyone who does not have God in his life is like a prisoner. Humanity's prison is sin. Jesus came to free you from this prison.

When Jesus unlocks the door for us, the devil cannot keep us inside his prison any longer. Then we are really free.

When you accept Jesus as your Savior and Redeemer, the doors of your prison open for you. I hope you have already been freed.

TWO ARE BETTER

Two are better than one. If one falls down,
his friend can help him up.
(Ecclesiastes 4:9, 10)

People were not made to be alone. People need each other. It's nice to know that when you are in trouble there is someone who will understand and who will not let you down.

The Bible says in Ecclesiastes that two are better than one. There are many things you cannot do alone. Someone can help you lift something heavy or explain school-work that you don't understand. On the sports field you can encourage and help one another.

Make friends with everyone who crosses your path. Then you will have friends that can support you. You can also mean a lot to them. It makes our lives meaningful. Thank God now for your friends and try to be a good friend to someone.

THINK THE RIGHT THOUGHTS

Set your minds on things above.
(Colossians 3:2)

Someone said that you are what you think. When you think nice thoughts, you become a nice person. On the other hand, if you think dirty and ugly thoughts, you become ugly in your actions also. Your thoughts are very important.

Every day thousands of thoughts come into our heads, even without our knowing about it. We must ask God to help us think the right thoughts. When the Holy Spirit lives in us He can help us. The Bible says we must think of things above. This means we must think about good and clean and noble things. This is what God thinks about.

If you catch yourself thinking something ugly, try to get a better thought immediately. Ask God to help you. I'm sure He will. May you have beautiful thoughts today.

LOVE YOUR PETS

... and Leviathan, which you made to play in the sea. (Psalm 104:26, NLT)

God must have enjoyed making all the different animals on earth. When I see how cute and interesting some of the animals are that He made, I cannot help thinking that God is wonderful. In Psalm 104 we read that God created an animal called a Leviathan to play in the sea.

Do you have a pet? People keep pets so that they can have a special animal to love and care for. In this way we learn that the animal kingdom is very important, and can also mean a lot to us humans.

When we have a pet we must thank God for it. We must take care of it with the love Jesus taught us. The love that Jesus puts in our hearts for humans and animals will be seen in the way we treat our pets. Glorify God through your care for your pet.

THE BEAUTIFUL GRAVE

"You are like whitewashed tombs, which look beautiful on the outside but on the inside are full of dead men's bones." (Matthew 23:27)

Have you been to a graveyard? There are usually beautiful flowers on the graves and also in gardens around the graves.

Many graves are beautifully decorated in expensive marble. On the marble slabs all kinds of nice things are written along with the name of the person buried there. But a person's body decays in that grave and later only bones are left.

Jesus warned that our lives must not look like graves. Outside someone can look beautiful while they are stone dead inside. By this the Bible means that we must live for Christ and that our hearts must be alive in this relationship with Him.

When you invite Jesus into your life, He lives inside you. Live for Jesus!

WHO HURTS YOU?

The men came after me and surrounded the house, intending to kill me. (Judges 20:5)

Many children are ill-treated, hurt and beaten by people who are very close to them. Others have someone who touches them in a way that is not right and who does bad things with them. We call this child abuse. It is a very bad thing to do, and children who experience this are unhappy.

Perhaps someone is hurting you in this way, or maybe you know of a friend who is being molested. What can you do?

Apart from telling God about your hurt, you must also get help. Speak to your youth leader or teacher and they will give you a number you can call where someone who understands will talk to you and help you.

A MIRACLE IN A CRISIS

And He touched the man's ear and healed him. (Luke 22:51)

Jesus went to the Garden of Gethsemane to pray for strength on the night before He was crucified. His Father had sent Him to die on the cross. That is why He asked God for help.

While Jesus was there, a lot of people arrived to capture Him. His disciple, Peter, pulled out his sword to defend Jesus and cut off a man's ear.

Although Jesus was in a crisis situation, He stretched out His hand and, with love in His heart, touched the man's ear and healed it. Isn't it wonderful that Jesus, in this moment of great crisis, still showed love and thought of others instead of just His own problems.

Jesus is never too busy to touch you with His love.

THE BACKUP PLAN

Sarai said to Abram, "Go, sleep with my maid-servant; perhaps I can build a family through her." Abram agreed to what Sarai said. (Genesis 16:2)

One night God made Abram look at the stars in the sky. He promised Abram that he would have just as many children as the stars in the sky. What God meant was that everybody who had a good relationship with Him would be children of Abram.

Abram and Sarai, his wife, were already old, and still they had no children. So Sarai told her husband to have a baby with her maidservant, Hagar. After all those years they didn't believe God's promise anymore, so they made a backup plan.

Our plans always make trouble if they are not God's will. Later on Abram and Sarai regretted this plan of theirs.

Making our own plans, without first talking to God, does not work.

JOSEPH CHOOSES GOD

"How then could I do such a wicked thing and sin against God?" (Genesis 39:9)

When Joseph was in a difficult situation in Potiphar's house, he had to make a choice. Instead of choosing to do something bad, he chose God.

You and I are often in situations where we must choose. You can choose to swear or not. You can choose to steal or not. You can choose if you want to gossip or not. Every day you and I can choose right or wrong, good or bad. We cannot make the right choice if we do not know what God's will is. That is why it is important to read His Word. We must also listen to His voice in our hearts. The Holy Spirit will help us make the right choices.

Tell God today that you want to choose Him. Ask His help to always make the right choices.

THE ANGEL NEXT TO YOU

For He will command His angels to guard you in all your ways. (Psalm 91:11)

The Bible says that God sends His angels to guard His children. Because Jesus is in heaven, He sent His Holy Spirit to be with us (John 14:16). But God also uses angels to be with people. Angels are heavenly beings, created to praise and glorify God and to carry out His instructions.

Because we can't see angels, we do not always realize how they help us. Angels are like strong winds or flames. They are big and strong and powerful. They can be with us in seconds, as they were with Daniel when they helped him in the lions' den.

You can be sure there is an angel guarding you today who will be with you everywhere you go. Thank God for His angels.

JESUS IS LIFE

"For the bread of God is He who comes down from heaven and gives life to the world." (John 6:33)

Many people have only bread to eat, but it keeps them alive. You probably like a sandwich with something tasty on it. We cannot survive without food.

The Bible says we cannot live on bread alone, however. God sent us His Son, the bread from heaven. He came so that we could have life. If we accept Jesus and believe in Him, and if we follow and serve Him, He is our bread that gives life.

You can eat delicious food and still be hungry in your heart. Only God can satisfy that hunger. Make sure that Jesus lives in you, and He will satisfy your hunger and give you life.

DON'T KEEP A RECORD

Love keeps no record of wrongs.
(1 Corinthians 13:5)

When we want to remember something, we often write it in a book, type it into a computer, or make a note of it on our calendars.

When we love someone, we should not write down all this person's faults and sins. We don't keep a record of faults.

Love does not make a list of someone's sins to take out at a later stage and use against that person. Love forgives and forgets all wrongs.

Maybe there is someone who wronged you. I hope you have forgotten about it. The best news is that Jesus does not keep a record of our sins. When we accepted Him, He washed us clean from sin. He forgets about our sins and frees us.

Let's forgive others as Jesus forgave us.

UNDER HIS FEET

"Sit at My right hand until I put your enemies under your feet." (Mark 12:36)

The enemy of God's kingdom is the devil. Jesus overcame the devil when He died on the cross and was raised from the dead. Now people can believe in Jesus and break loose from the devil.

Unfortunately, the devil has not been defeated completely. He hurts many people and leads them astray to follow him.

A day will come when God will have the devil completely under His control and will destroy him once and for all. At that time, whoever did good things and followed Jesus will be rewarded. The others will go with the devil. Jesus will rule forever and ever. The devil will be under His feet and have no more influence.

Until Jesus finally rules over the devil, we must faithfully follow in Jesus' footsteps.

BEING FAITHFUL

But the fruit of the Spirit is ... faithfulness.
(Galatians 5:22)

Faithfulness means that we can rely on something or someone. This is very important in life. When you sit on a chair, you trust that it will not collapse under you. If the doctor gives you medicine, you trust it will make you better. If you cannot trust someone, you will always be suspicious that they might do something you won't like.

Often people tell us they will do something and then they don't. This is not a nice thing to happen. The Holy Spirit wants to help us to be trustworthy in everything we do and keep our promises. Even when no one sees, we must still be faithful because the Holy Spirit encourages us to do the right thing.

Ask the Holy Spirit to fill you today and to make you faithful in everything you do.

IT HURTS TO BE SHARPENED

As iron sharpens iron, so one person sharpens another. (Proverbs 27:17)

Have you ever seen someone sharpen a knife? Most people hold it against a grindstone. It must be painful to be rubbed so hard. Luckily, a knife and a grindstone can't feel a thing.

Humans get hurt easily. As a knife rubs against a grindstone, people also sometimes rub against one another. It's just like when a river rolls a stone around, bumping it against other stones to become another shape.

The Bible says we sharpen or polish one another in the same way. We don't always like it when people differ from us. When we humans clash, we shape one another. What others say and think of you can sometimes hurt, but once the truth is out, you can just give it a better shape.

Allow God to shape you in His way.

A TOE OR A PINKIE

Now you are the body of Christ, and each one of you is a part of it.
(1 Corinthians 12:27)

When you belong to Jesus, you are part of His wonderful body, a body of Christians. Each person has many body parts like a nose, eyes, ears, legs, arms and toes. Every body part has something special to do, but they all need each other to form a whole.

Every Christian has a place in the large body of Jesus. We need one another. Each of us also has a task. God has a plan for each and every one of us so that His whole body can work together wonderfully well. Never think you are not valuable. The Lord wants to use you; He needs you.

Thank God right now that you can be part of His body, and ask Him to use you just as He pleases.

SMOKE IN YOUR EYES

As smoke to the eyes, so is a sluggard to those who send him. (Proverbs 10:26)

Have you ever sat at a fire somewhere in the open? It creates a cozy atmosphere. But if you sit on the wrong side of the fire, the smoke gets in your eyes. It burns your eyes. Soon your eyes water and you can't see much. It is very unpleasant.

This is the image the Bible uses to tell us how it feels to work with a lazy person. Lazy is the opposite of diligent. A diligent person is hard working and zealous. A diligent child is not afraid of work. A diligent child enjoys helping others. When you give a diligent child something to do, he does it with a smile because it is no trouble to him. Lazy children and lazy grown-ups are like smoke in the eyes.

Be diligent today and enjoy doing something for someone else.

CARRYING YOUR CROSS

*"And anyone who does not carry his cross
and follow Me cannot be My disciple."*
(Luke 14:27)

There are people who think that to carry a cross means to have a hard time and to suffer. Jesus carried His cross.

When Jesus tells us, His disciples, to take up our cross, it does not mean we must carry a cross in the way that He did. It simply means that we must be prepared to follow Him. To follow Jesus is to do what He asks us and to obey what He says.

In Jesus' time the cross was a sign of disgrace. Only bad people were nailed to a cross. But to you and me the cross is a wonderful sign, because it is on the cross that Jesus died for our sins. Let's tell Him that we are very happy, and let's tell others that we are prepared to follow Him.

CALL THE DOCTOR

"It is not the healthy who need a doctor, but the sick." (Mark 2:17)

When we are sick, our parents watch us closely, and if we don't get better, they take us to see the doctor. Doctors study a long time to help sick people get better. We can thank the Lord for doctors and pray for them.

Luke was a doctor. Jesus used the image of a doctor to tell people why He came to live on earth. Jesus came to heal sick people. Not only illnesses of the body, but especially of the soul.

Everyone who lives far away from God is sick in their relationship with the Lord. Jesus came down to earth for lost, sinful people. The Bible says through His wounds we are healed.

Be honest about your spiritual illness and ask the Lord to heal your heart.

THE MOST IMPORTANT

... so that you may be able to discern what is best. (Philippians 1:10)

Something we have to learn in life is to know what is the most important. If you are taking a test tomorrow, then you know it is important that you study today.

To know what is important, more important, and even most important, requires the ability to discern.

This means we must be able to tell one thing from another. The Lord helps us to sense things so that we are able to tell the important from the more important in our spiritual lives.

It is more important to have a good relationship with Jesus Christ than to be popular with the world. Maybe the most important is to know that your sins have been forgiven. May the Lord teach you through the Holy Spirit which things are the most important.

THE APPLE OF HIS EYE

For whoever touches you touches the apple of His eye. (Zechariah 2:8)

Some people think they are not good enough for the Lord. They see their faults, and they think the Lord will never be satisfied with them. Yet the Lord redeemed them and calls them His children. When we are the Lord's children, He loves us so much that we can say we are the apple of His eye.

One's eye is a very sensitive organ. When something gets into your eye, you feel it immediately and try to get it out quickly. Also, one cannot touch a person's eye, because it is very, very sensitive. Our eyes are very precious because we see with them. That is why we take very good care of our eyes. If the Lord says that we are the apple of His eye, it means that we are very precious to Him. Remember today that you are very special and that you are the apple of God's eye.

WITH OPEN ARMS

"Let the little children come to Me, and do not hinder them." (Matthew 19:14)

When Jesus was on earth, some people thought He was so important and so busy that He did not have time for children. Fortunately, this was not true. The Lord loves children very much. To tell the truth, He said if we don't become like children we will never enter the kingdom of heaven.

The Lord's heart beats warmly for children. He wants to be with them. He understands how they feel. He wants to guide them, teach them, and show them how to become happy grown-ups – and how to be happy children!

When the disciples wanted to stop the mothers from bringing their children to Jesus, Jesus welcomed the children.

God also loves you. He understands and cares for you. You will always feel welcome with Jesus.

HEART TRANSPLANT

"I will give you a new heart and put a new spirit in you ... " (Ezekiel 36:26)

Some babies are born with bad hearts. They need urgent medical help. There are also grown-ups that develop heart problems at a later stage in their lives. Some develop such a bad heart that they must get a new one. We call this a heart transplant. It means that doctors put a healthy heart into a person with a sick heart. There is then new hope for the sick patient. The Lord is also like a doctor who does heart transplants.

You and I also have bad hearts. Our hearts are full of sin, so we need new ones. Only Jesus can give you a new heart.

It is very important that we exchange our old hearts for new ones. We don't have to lie on an operating table; the Lord does the operation quietly and without fuss when we tell Him that we need a new heart.

STONE OR FLESH?

"I will remove from them their heart of stone and give them a heart of flesh."
(Ezekiel 11:19)

The Bible says we must get a new heart because sin has made our hearts as hard as stone. Sin makes you look at things differently from what the Lord would like you to. It turns us into unhappy people and causes us to hurt others very easily.

The Lord tells us to give our hearts of stone to Him, and He will exchange them for hearts of flesh. Flesh can be cut with a knife, but stone can't. The Lord asks you and me to give our hearts to Him. He will make our hearts soft, so that we can live better lives, act better, and just be nicer people.

Have you asked for a heart of flesh yet? Let's ask the Lord to help us even more to become soft-hearted.

MOTHERS ARE WONDERFUL

A woman who fears the LORD is to be praised. (Proverbs 31:30)

Mothers are wonderful. They look after us when we are not well, they help us when we don't understand things and they comfort us when we are unhappy.

How often do you think about all the good things your mother does for you each day? Just imagine if your mother had to go away for a day or two. Who would do all the things she does for you? Whom would you go to if you were upset about something that happened at school? Who would prepare your lunch for school? These things wouldn't be the same without your mom, would they?

Remember to pray a special prayer each day thanking God for your mother, and asking Him to help you appreciate her more. Ask the Lord to help you to make it easy for your mom to look after you.

TALK TO THE LORD

If you have anything to say speak up, for I want you to be cleared. (Job 33:32)

Sometimes we do not feel like speaking to anyone. Especially when we are feeling sad and we think no one will understand, we don't want to talk. Perhaps your mother sees that you are unhappy and then says to you, "Tell me what is wrong. Talk to me!" Yes, it is better to talk about it. It is better to say how you feel. When you have talked about it you will start feeling better. To bottle up all your feelings and say nothing is not a good thing at all.

Because the Lord knows this, He wants you to talk to Him.

Are there things in your heart that no one knows about? Talk to God about it.

HE LISTENS

His ear is not too dull to hear. (Isaiah 59:1)

Some people can't hear because they are deaf. Something is wrong with their ears, and they can't process sounds.

There are also those who do not want to hear. They can, but they choose not to. Sometimes when you speak to people they are thinking of other things, and they don't hear you. Or they ignore you.

The Lord invites us to speak to Him. He wants us to open up our hearts to Him and tell Him everything that is going on in our lives and what we are keeping ourselves busy with. He invites us to speak to Him, and He will listen to us; He wants to.

God listens to everything we say or think. He is never too busy to take notice of you and listen to you. He never ignores you. His thoughts are never someplace else. Isn't it wonderful! He is listening to you.

THE SHORT ARM

Surely the arm of the LORD is not too short to save. (Isaiah 59:1)

People in Old Testament times thought that God was far away. He was somewhere in the clouds of heaven. He was not yet Immanuel, God with us. Jesus had not come down to earth yet. That is why they always prayed that God must help them. Maybe they thought, "How can God help us if He is so far away? Maybe He has a long arm so that He can help us here on earth even if He lives in heaven."

Of course they were making a mistake. God is not only in heaven. He is everywhere. He can help anyone on earth in a second.

I know that God can and will help us; we are His children when we believe in Christ. He has come very close to us, through Jesus and the Holy Spirit. If you need help, ask God right now to help you.

BAD SPIRITS

For our struggle is not against flesh and blood, but ... against the spiritual forces of evil in the heavenly realms. (Ephesians 6:12)

The Holy Spirit is with us. He is our helper and the Comforter.

The devil managed to get a lot of angels on his side, and he took them with him when he left heaven. They became bad. These evil spirits are the servants of the devil, and they attack people and want to destroy them. When Jesus was on earth He drove a lot of evil spirits out of people's hearts. Some of them screamed as they left a person, because they were afraid of Jesus. Jesus came to put an end to the work of the devil.

If we belong to Jesus, the Holy Spirit lives in us and we do not have to be afraid of evil spirits. The best thing to do, really, is to ignore them. A heart that is full of the Holy Spirit and Jesus has nothing to be afraid of.

GOODBYE JESUS

After He said this, He was taken up before
their very eyes, and a cloud hid Him.
(Acts 1:9)

Ascension Day is the day we celebrate Jesus being taken into heaven.

When Jesus' work on earth was finished, He went to His Father in heaven. I would imagine that God was very pleased to see Jesus. The angels and the Father were probably cheering Jesus when He got to heaven after suffering for us. He conquered death. He is the Winner, and that is why everyone in heaven must have received Him with such joy. He then got a name above all other names.

Now Jesus is in heaven to plead with God for you and me. He prays for us when we are in trouble. He sends the angels to help us. He also went to prepare a place for us. Thank Jesus that He went to prepare a place for us.

THE VOICE BEHIND YOU

"Whether you turn to the right or to the left, your ears will hear a voice behind you, saying, 'This is the way; walk in it.'"
(Isaiah 30:21)

When you are on your way somewhere and you are not sure of the road, you sometimes make a wrong decision and lose your way. When people travel by car to places far away, there are sometimes forks in the road (one road turns left and the other to the right). How do they know which one to take? There are road maps to help, or someone will show them the way.

God wants to direct us and show us the right way. The Bible says we will hear a voice behind us that will tell us if we should turn left or right. Of course it will not be the same as hearing one another's voices. God's voice cannot be heard; He speaks through His Word and His Spirit.

Listen to God's voice: He will direct you.

MILK OR MEAT?

I gave you milk, not solid food, for you were not yet ready for it. (1 Corinthians 3:2)

Three-day-old babies cannot eat a hamburger. Little babies can only drink milk because they have not developed enough to eat solids yet. When you have given your life to Jesus you are like a little baby in faith. You don't understand enough of what is written in the Bible. Someone must teach you about God's Word.

As a baby grows, he gets stronger. Quite soon this baby needs more than milk. Then his mom or dad gives him veggies and meat, and when he is older, he can eat grilled meat when the family has a cookout. The same goes for you and me. First we were babies in our faith, but we learned more and more about the Word of God.

I hope you have finished with milk and are now eating the delicious, grilled meat of God's Word.

TEN GOLDEN RULES

And God spoke all these words.
(Exodus 20:1)

When the people of God were taken out of Egypt, the Lord gave them the Ten Commandments. He did this to help them so that they would know how He wanted them to live. If they kept these commandments, all would be well and they would be happy. God's Ten Commandments were like golden rules that helped them love one another and do things the right way.

Because we are sinners and make mistakes, the Lord must teach us how to live. We can read the Ten Commandments because they will help us do the right thing.

The Holy Spirit, who lives in our hearts, makes us willing to keep God's commandments. Let's do what the Lord wants. Only a fool would think that what God says is not important.

ENJOY LIFE

Young people, it's wonderful to be young! Enjoy every minute of it. Do everything you want to do; take it all in. But remember that you must give an account to God for everything you do. (Ecclesiastes 11:9, NLT)

You're only young once, and when you are young, there are many things that are important to you. The Lord wants you to enjoy your youth. We all have different interests. There are things that you enjoy more than someone else would. Maybe you like TV games, sports, or hobbies. Perhaps you like riding your skateboard, going to the movies, or visiting friends. Perhaps you like nothing better than playing football or singing. Whatever you like, or whatever you want to do, the Bible says to enjoy it.

We can really enjoy our lives only if we do things the way Jesus would. The Lord will help us, and His Holy Spirit will show us how.

GOD WORKS WITH A FEW

"With the three hundred men, I will save you." (Judges 7:7)

God told Gideon to get the Israelites together to fight against Midian. They got together twenty-two thousand very brave Israelite soldiers. But God said He did not want that many. Too many? Against the many soldiers of Midian they were just a handful. How could God say there were too many of them!

The reason for using so few men against Midian is that the Lord wanted to show very clearly that it was not the power of Israel that would bring them victory, but the power of God. When God wants to win, He can use anything. How much you and I can do is not important. It all depends on His great strength. With God on your side, you can come out on top. Ask Him to help you.

WHOM DO YOU TRUST?

No one needed to tell Him about human nature, for He knew what was in each person's heart. (John 2:25, NLT)

People often disappoint us. We put our trust in someone, and then that person does not do what he said he would. It would be a pity if we feel we can never trust anyone ever again, because we all need one another in life.

Jesus didn't trust just anybody. We read in the Bible that when Jesus was in Jerusalem for the Feast of the Passover, many people started believing in Him when they saw the miracles He did. The Bible also says that He didn't put His trust in them, because He knew all about people (see verse 24).

You and I must learn from Jesus. We must never put our complete trust in people. We should rather trust God with all our hearts.

THE SHORT MAN

He wanted to see who Jesus was, but being a short man he could not, because of the crowd. (Luke 19:3)

Zacchaeus was a rich and important man in his town. But because he was short, he could not see Jesus passing by in the midst of the crowds. So he climbed in a tree.

When Jesus passed underneath the tree, He looked up and said, "Zacchaeus, come down immediately. I must stay at your house today" (Luke 19:5). When he got over the shock, Zacchaeus invited Jesus to his house. Some of the religious people were upset. They thought it was wrong of Jesus to visit the house of a sinner. But Jesus had a plan for Zacchaeus's life.

We must also go to people's houses, visit with them , and tell them about Jesus' love and forgiveness. Maybe it will work a miracle in their lives.

NEARLY, BUT NOT QUITE

"Do you think that in such a short time you can persuade me to be a Christian?"
(Acts 26:28)

Paul was imprisoned by the Jews because he followed Jesus. They brought him before King Agrippa of the Roman Empire. He had heard about this Jesus and wanted to know more about Him. So he asked Paul about Jesus and why he followed Him.

Paul explained everything about Jesus' life on earth and how He came to set up His kingdom. Agrippa listened carefully. Agrippa told Paul, "You are almost convincing me to become a Christian."

Many people are almost Christians. They believe in Jesus and the Bible with half a heart. Still, they don't get around to accepting Him. You and I should, like Paul, go on telling them it is worthwhile to follow Jesus with your whole heart.

THE BAD WOMAN

He married Jezebel and began to serve Baal and worship him. (1 Kings 16:31)

King Ahab was a king of Israel. Unfortunately, he was not a very good king because he did what was wrong in the eyes of God. One of the big mistakes he made was to marry a woman who did not love God. Her name was Jezebel. She was a heathen, and she worshiped a god named Baal.

Jezebel tried to kill the prophets of God. She took care of a few hundred false prophets that served Baal. She wanted to lure the people of Israel away from the Lord, and she also wanted to kill Elijah.

There are people today who do not want to do the will of God. Some of them are leaders. Like Jezebel, they are trying to sabotage the work of the Lord. We must pray for bad people like Jezebel and show them that it is better to serve the Lord.

THE COMFORTER

"He will give you another Counselor ... the Spirit of truth." (John 14:16, 17)

A counselor is also a comforter. Has anyone ever comforted you? Of course! When we hurt ourselves, or something bad happens in our lives, it is wonderful to have someone who comforts us. A comforter is someone who says, "Never mind, things will get better."

The Lord knows that we, the people on earth, suffer. That is why He sent us a Comforter. The Comforter's name is the Holy Spirit. He lives in the hearts of everyone who has accepted Jesus. The Holy Spirit is wonderful. He comforts us in difficult times. He encourages us. He inspires us and motivates us.

Are you hurting because of someone or something? Then you should ask the Holy Spirit to comfort you.

THE RIGHT SHOES

*... with your feet fitted with the readiness
that comes from the gospel of peace.
(Ephesians 6:15)*

We know that soldiers who fight a battle must wear the right shoes. They cannot go to war barefoot. They would not be able to fight properly. The Bible uses the image to say that we also need the right "shoes" when we face battles with the devil.

The image of the shoes that the Bible mentions is the preparedness to talk about Jesus. As a soldier puts on the right shoes for the battle, we, as children of the Lord, must also wear the right shoes. We must be prepared to tell others about Jesus, and we must be prepared to live for Him.

Are you prepared to tell others about Jesus? If not, get prepared today. In this way, good soldiers win the war.

THE DOVE

Heaven was opened and the Holy Spirit descended on Him in bodily form like a dove. (Luke 3:21-22)

The dove is a symbol of peace. Perhaps you have seen how doves are released at important gatherings. It is truly beautiful to see them fly in the blue sky. The soft cooing of a dove brings peace to the soul. Doves are not birds of prey. Doves are not aggressive. Doves are friendly birds.

When Jesus was baptized, the Holy Spirit descended on Him in the form of a dove. It must have been beautiful to see. The Holy Spirit enabled Jesus to do His work. Jesus is called the Prince of Peace. Yes, the Holy Spirit brings peace for you and me through the Prince of Peace, Jesus Christ. When the Holy Spirit lives in us, we also have peace in our hearts. Ask the Lord to fill you with the peace of His Spirit.

YOU ARE A HOUSE

Do you not know that your body is a
temple of the Holy Spirit, who is in you?
(1 Corinthians 6:19)

In the Old Testament the people of Israel built the Lord a place where they could meet with Him. They called it the house of God, the temple, tabernacle, or place of assembly. But the Lord does not live in manmade buildings anymore. When Jesus came to earth, He decided to live in a new home: our bodies.

It sounds almost too good to be true. How can the mighty God of heaven and earth live in our bodies? When we accept the Lord, He comes to live inside us. That is why the Bible calls our bodies, yours and mine, the temple of the Holy Spirit.

Because the mighty, wonderful Lord lives inside you and me, we must look after our bodies.

LET HIM GUIDE YOU

"But when He, the Spirit of truth, comes, He will guide you into all truth." (John 16:13)

Have you ever seen someone lead a blind person? A blind person cannot see. That is why someone takes his hand and leads him in the right direction.

The Bible tells us in Romans 8:14 that the Spirit guides the children of God. This means that He shows us the right way. He shows us where to walk, what to do, how to act. He leads us in the truth. This is not just about church on Sunday or Sunday school. It is all about our thoughts, how we practice sports, how we relax, how we do our schoolwork. The Holy Spirit wants to teach us how to behave in every situation. He leads us in the truth of God's Word.

When the Holy Spirit is our Guide, we can be sure that we will always have the peace of the Lord in our hearts.

A STAMMERED PRAYER

He beat his breast and said, "God, have mercy on me, a sinner." (Luke 18:13)

Jesus told a parable about two men who went to the temple to pray. When these two men got to the temple, they acted differently. One was a Pharisee. This meant he had a very important position in the church. The other was a tax collector. Tax collectors were not good people. They did not have a good reputation. When the Pharisee prayed, he thanked the Lord that he was good, and not bad, like the tax collector. This Pharisee was haughty and his heart was filled with pride. The Lord does not like this. The tax collector, on the other hand, felt very bad. He knew he was nothing but a sinner. He begged for forgiveness and asked the Lord to have mercy on him.

Jesus said that the prayer of the tax collector was the best one. You and I must also be humble before the Lord.

SOW THE SEED

"A farmer went out to sow his seed."
(Matthew 13:3)

Farmers plow a piece of land and then sow seed in that land so that it can come up and bear fruit. Some of the seed the farmer plants does not come up. Maybe that seed landed in the wrong place.

The Lord said that His gospel is like seed that falls to the ground. Every Christian is like a farmer who sows seed. You and I must try to sow God's seed in the lives of people. Wherever we go, we can tell people about God and explain His Word to them. This is seed that can come up in people's hearts and bear fruit that will make God happy.

Sometimes the seed falls on hard soil. This is like a person with a hard heart who doesn't want to accept God's Word. Sow good seeds today, wherever you go.

"STORM BE STILL"

He got up and rebuked the wind and the raging waters. (Luke 8:24)

One day Jesus and His disciples got into a boat, and Jesus told them to go over to the other side of the lake. While they were sailing, Jesus fell asleep. He must have been very tired. A heavy storm broke over the lake, and water came into the boat. Soon they were in danger of sinking. They woke Jesus up. They asked Him to help quickly; the boat was sinking.

Jesus got up and did an interesting thing: He spoke sternly to the wind. The waves died down and there was peace. It was a miracle. Just by talking, Jesus calmed the storm.

If you have problems, the Lord can also speak one word, and your life can change. Trust Him with your problems. Ask Him to help, He will take care of you.

NOT LITTLE, BUT LOTS

They all ate and were satisfied, and the disciples picked up twelve basketfuls of broken pieces. (Luke 9:17)

O nce Jesus preached near the Sea of Galilee. The crowds were hanging on His every word. The day passed quickly, and the people became hungry.

In the book of Luke we read that a little boy brought Jesus two fish and five loaves of bread. Jesus looked up to heaven, said grace, and started passing the bread around. Thousands ate, and still there was food left over!

You and I must make sure that what we have is available to the Lord so that He can use it. The two fish and five loaves were good enough for the Lord to perform a miracle. Bring what you have to the Lord – your life, talents, time, money – and see Him work a miracle with it.

ON THIS ROCK

"On this rock I will build My church."
(Matthew 16:18)

One day Jesus gave Simon, son of Jonah, a new name. Jesus wanted to change his name to Peter, because he had a special plan for Peter's life. Peter means "rock."

Jesus gave Peter this name after asking what people were saying about Him. People were talking behind Jesus' back. But was it the truth? That is why Jesus asked this question. The reply was that people said He was a great prophet like Elijah. When Jesus asked His disciples who they thought He was, Peter answered that He was the Redeemer and the Anointed One, that He was the Son of God. This answer pleased Jesus and He said, "On this rock I will build My church" (Matthew 16:18). What Peter said is true, and if we believe it, we are building the kingdom of Jesus.

YOUR LIFE IS PRECIOUS

"What good will it be for a man if he gains the whole world, yet forfeits his soul?"
(Matthew 16:26)

Jesus says that our lives are very precious. That is why we protect ourselves. That is why we look after ourselves when we are ill. That is why we are afraid of criminals and murderers; they can destroy our lives.

Jesus teaches us that the best thing you can do to protect your life is to give it to Him. You can be selfish and keep your life to yourself. You don't want to give your heart and your life to Jesus. Jesus warns that if you think you are going to keep or protect your life in this way, you are definitely going to lose it. If we open up our hearts and give our lives to the Lord, then we will have true life.

Decide today that you would rather follow Jesus – lose your life in Him so that you can gain your life back.

SIN IS SIN

For whoever keeps the whole law and yet stumbles at just one point is guilty of breaking all of it. (James 2:10)

There is no such thing as small sins and big sins. We think it is not such a big sin if we steal something small; we will be forgiven easily. But murder is a big thing, and maybe we won't be forgiven for that. It does not work like that in God's eyes.

Sinning means that we fail. If we fail in a big or a small way, we still fail. The Lord says stealing a pencil is just as bad as committing a murder. Sin is sin.

We will forgive something small quite readily, but whenever a big sin is committed to us, it is very difficult to forgive. God forgives us if we confess our sins, whether it's a big or a small sin.

Let's thank the Lord that He is willing to forgive all sins. But let's try not to sin.

BUILD THE TEMPLE

"Not by might nor by power, but by My Spirit," says the LORD Almighty.
(Zechariah 4:6)

The Lord sent His people back to Jerusalem to rebuild the temple. But the people were not up to this task. How were they to rebuild the temple? The Lord answered them in a vision. He showed Zechariah how they could build: not with might and power, but by the Spirit of the Lord. Zechariah told Zerubbabel, the man who had to build the temple, that all he had to do was get started with the guidance of the Holy Spirit. The Holy Spirit would give him the courage to do the work, and provide building material.

Zerubbabel got started, and everything happened like Zechariah said it would. Maybe you also have a task that is getting you down. Ask the Holy Spirit to help you. If it is God's will, you will succeed.

DEEP IN YOUR HEART

*People may be pure in their own eyes, but
the LORD examines their motives.*
(Proverbs 16:2, NLT)

We see the outside of people. We see someone laugh, being happy or friendly. It could be that this person is being friendly because he wants something from you. His motives are not quite honest, but you don't notice it at first.

It can also happen that someone seems angry. For example, a teacher may be very strict with you or with your class. Deep in her heart she may have a sincere wish to help you, and that is the reason for her behavior. Her motives are good.

The Lord does not look at the outside. He looks into the heart. He knows what our motives are. He knows exactly why we do things.

Serve the Lord because you really love Him. Serve Him for the right reasons.

THE RIGHT WORDS

How good is a timely word! (Proverbs 15:23)

Words carry a message. What we say has a meaning. If you say there is a snake in the house, you are communicating a fact. Then everybody gets afraid. If you say a flower is pretty, you say it because you see a pretty flower and you want others to see it too.

Words can also be used in the wrong way. Sometimes we say one thing and mean another. We must learn to use language correctly.

We need wisdom to say the right words at the right time. Let's ask the Lord to help us. I have learned that the Holy Spirit helps me to say the right things. Still, I must also, same as you, ask the Lord to help me so that I don't say the wrong thing.

WORK HARD

Diligent hands bring wealth. (Proverbs 10:4)

Being diligent means to always work hard. It is the opposite of being lazy. Diligent people know that there is work to do and do it. They don't sleep too late. When they are working, they do not allow their thoughts to be busy with other things. They are disciplined. They have realized that hard work is good for them.

The Bible says that one gets rich if one is diligent. If we work hard, the Lord will bless our work. Lazy people usually have a hard time being successful.

Someone who is not afraid to use his hands is someone who always has bread on the table. I hope you are diligent. Do your homework diligently. Help your mom in the house. Don't be lazy. Then you will also be one of those people who always have enough in life.

REFRESHING OTHERS

He who refreshes others will himself be refreshed. (Proverbs 11:25)

There are so many needy people around us. There are hungry people. There are thirsty people. There are people who need clothes. There are people who need love. There are people who need friendship. Yes, and there are people with a "thirst" in their hearts.

We often think our own needs are so important that we cannot afford to help others. Sometimes we are stingy with what we have, and we don't want to share with others. The Bible teaches us an important lesson: you and I should be more eager to give than to receive. If you and I have learned this great lesson, all will be well in our lives.

Don't be stingy. Give to others, and you will also receive.

WORDS LIKE SILVER

The words of the LORD are flawless, like silver. (Psalm 12:6)

We sometimes say things that we don't really mean.

If you said you would do something and you didn't, your words were false. You lied. Your words meant nothing; they were just sounds. We must try to do what we promise.

Sometimes something comes up and we can't keep our promises. But we must really try not to speak false words. If we compliment someone on a pretty dress or a good voice, it must come from the heart. We must mean what we say.

There is someone whose words are never false: the Lord. What He says is true. His words are like genuine silver.

THE BEST

He found none equal to Daniel, Hananiah, Mishael and Azariah; so they entered the king's service. (Daniel 1:19)

God wants to be proud of His children. We must do our best and use the talents He has given us.

In the time of King Nebuchadnezzar there were four men who knew the Lord and served Him. The Bible says that God gave these men intelligence and also insight into everything they learned. They lived the way the Lord prescribed. That is why they didn't eat the king's food and drink his wine. They ate only healthy food as they had been doing since childhood. That is why they looked healthier.

When we serve the Lord, He uses us, just like Daniel and his friends. What the Lord prescribes is always best.

ADVICE FOR THE KING

Be pleased to accept my advice: Renounce your sins by doing what is right ... then your prosperity will continue. (Daniel 4:27)

God loved Daniel very much and wanted to use him, even in a heathen country. That is why God gave Daniel the ability to interpret or explain dreams. One night King Nebuchadnezzar had a dream that upset him. His advisers could not interpret the dream. Then the Lord helped Daniel to interpret the king's dream.

Daniel explained the dream and gave the king a message. Daniel was only a servant, but he gave the Lord's message to the king, loud and clear. The king had to stop sinning and doing things that were wrong. But the king didn't listen to Daniel. He went on doing bad things.

You and I must give people the Lord's messages faithfully and respectfully as Daniel did.

SHUTTING THE LIONS' MOUTHS

They brought Daniel and threw him into the lions' den. (Daniel 6:16)

Daniel's enemies plotted against him. They knew that Daniel prayed to God three times a day. So they went and asked the king to forbid the people to worship anybody but King Darius.

Because Daniel worshiped only God, they captured him and threw him into a lions' den. But God protected Daniel by sending His angel to shut the mouths of the lions. The king was very glad that the lions hadn't eaten Daniel, because he loved Daniel very much.

King Darius realized that the people had been scheming against Daniel, and he ordered that the guilty ones be thrown into the lions' den instead.

No matter who makes wicked plans against you, the Lord will help you out. Just trust Him and be faithful like Daniel.

WAIT FOR STRENGTH

Those who hope in the LORD will renew their strength. (Isaiah 40:31)

When you walk far, your legs get tired and weak, and it feels as if you have no more strength left. Then you must take a rest to renew your strength.

Your spirit can also get tired. We usually say a person who is tired in his or her spirit is depressed or despondent. There are many people around us who are so depressed they don't even want to live any more. The Lord teaches us how we can get strength back into our spirit.

He says if we are despondent or feel weak, we must first be still. We must wait for Him. We must quiet down our hearts. By reading the Bible and speaking to the Lord, we will get new strength from Him.

I WANT IT!

An inheritance quickly gained ... will not be blessed at the end. (Proverbs 20:21)

There are things you want and don't always get. Yet you keep on thinking about them. You want them so badly that you nag your parents. You even ask the Lord to give you what you want.

It is not wrong to want certain things. Just make sure that things are not more important to you than people or God. If we want something badly, it is not wrong to ask the Lord. When I was a young boy there was something I wanted very badly. For quite a few months I wished I could have it; I even asked the Lord for it. When I gave up hope, the Lord gave it to me in a wonderful way, through an aunt and an uncle. The Lord sometimes gives us our heart's desire.

Tell the Lord your wishes, and leave the matter in His hands.

ADVICE FOR THE YOUNG

How can a young person stay pure? By obeying Your word. (Psalm 119:9, NLT)

Young people are precious to the Lord. He wants to give them the best. His Word also speaks to young people. It is important to the Lord that young people keep their lives pure. If you are unclean in your youth, then you become a dirty grown-up. And you pass that dirt on to your children. When are you dirty in God's eyes? When sin has become a habit in your life.

Many young people are caught up in the web of sin. They are destroying their lives. It hurts them, breaks them, and makes them dirty and sad.

The Lord says a young person can keep his or her life pure in one way only: when he or she lives according to the Lord's Word. If we do what He wants, our lives will be pure.

WHAT REMAINS?

"The earth ... and the heavens ... will perish,
but You remain." (Hebrews 1:10, 11)

It's too bad that fun things don't last forever. A holiday is fun, but it passes so quickly. That delicious chocolate is finished before you know it. You wish you had more, but it is all gone. It is the same with life. Here on earth nothing lasts forever.

The Bible says God made heaven and earth. There are so many wonderful things on earth to enjoy. But these things pass.

Only God will be there forever. That is why we should belong to Him and He must be our Lord. We will never lose Him. He is always there. He lives forever, and if we love Him, we will live with Him forever.

BARE TREES

They are like trees in autumn that are doubly dead, for they bear no fruit and have been pulled up by the roots. (Jude 1:12, NLT)

Some people plant fruit trees in their gardens so that they can enjoy delicious fruit. They don't just plant the tree, they water it and fertilize it so that the fruit will be good. They wait the whole season for the fruit to ripen so that they can enjoy it.

It sometimes happens that the fruit of a tree is disappointing, in spite of the fact that it was cared for. Instead of nice ripe fruit, there is sometimes no fruit at all, or the fruit does not taste good. What a disappointment! There are also people who don't bear good fruit. They are like dead trees that bear no fruit.

You must start bearing fruit when you are still young. This is how you praise the name of the Lord.

RICH AND POOR ARE EQUAL

Rich and poor have this in common: The LORD is the Maker of them all.
(Proverbs 22:2)

It is typical of people to look down on those who are not as well off as they are. The rich sometimes have too much pride in their hearts and think a homeless person or someone who is very poor is not important. They think they are more important just because they have more money.

How fortunate we are that the Lord does not see us in that way. He doesn't mind if we are rich or poor. It does not matter to Him how important we are in the eyes of people. It does not matter to Him how much money we have in the bank. He doesn't even care if we are good-looking or ugly. He loves us just the way we are. He loves rich and poor – we're all equal in His eyes. Ask the Lord to help you love all people equally like He does.

SUN-SCORCHED AND DRY

The LORD will guide you always; He will satisfy your needs in a sun-scorched land. (Isaiah 58:11)

Israel is a very dry country. There are parts that are barren, just like a desert. In the time of the Bible there were no cars. People had to walk where they wanted to go. It was a slow way to travel, and they usually had some pack animal with them. In such a dry and barren place there is very little water. It is also usually very hot in a desert.

Our lives sometimes go through dry and barren patches. This means that things don't always go well for us. Sometimes you go through bad times, and you seem to be walking through a barren, sun-scorched desert. It could be that your mom and dad are getting divorced. You could be ill. Or you could be in some trouble at school. This makes you unhappy. Just trust Him.

I GIVE BACK

"Whose ox have I taken? Whom have I cheated? ... I will make it right."
(1 Samuel 12:3)

Sometimes it's just not good enough to say you're sorry. You must also give back. If you have borrowed someone's pen and it broke, you must be willing to give that person a new one. If you have taken something from someone by accident, you must give it back. If you pick up something that someone has lost, you must try and find the owner.

When Samuel came to the end of his life, he wanted to make sure that he did not have anything with him that belonged to another person. That is why he asked if he owed anyone anything. He wanted to set matters straight and give back. He wanted nobody to blame him for something he had not returned.

FIRST ASK

He inquired of the LORD. Once again David inquired of the LORD. (1 Samuel 23:2, 4)

David was king of Israel. He had to fight the Philistines. The Philistines wanted to kill the Israelites. The Bible says that David inquired of the Lord. When you inquire about something, you ask about it. This means we must become quiet before the Lord. We must go to one side and speak to the Lord. We must pray, and we must also listen. We believe that He will give us wisdom. That is why we ask Him.

Often something comes up in our thoughts and we decide that it is exactly what we want to do. We don't really ask anyone. Nor do we tell someone that we plan to do it. We just decide to do it. The safest way is to do what David did: first ask the Lord. Then we will not make so many mistakes.

LIKE A FLEA

"Why has the king of Israel come out to search for a single flea? Why does he hunt me down like a partridge on the mountains?" (1 Samuel 26:20, NLT)

Saul was the first king of Israel. He sinned against God, and the Lord renounced him. Saul tried to kill David. Saul and a few of his men went after David. David fled into the mountains and hid in caves.

Yet, David was not bitter toward Saul. He trusted in the Lord. He still respected Saul because the Lord had made him king of Israel. There were times when David could have killed Saul, but he didn't. One day he was very close to Saul, and this is when he said he was like a flea, a tiny partridge that lives in the mountains. David's humility was so sincere that Saul felt sick at heart, "I have sinned ... I will not try to harm you again." (verse 21). Saul did not keep his promise, but the Lord kept David safe.

THE LORD LIVES

The LORD lives! Praise be to my Rock!
(Psalm 18:46)

Jesus died on the cross for our sins. When He breathed His last, His spirit passed into the hands of His Father. Then Jesus was taken down from the cross. He was dead. They wrapped His broken body in a clean linen cloth. Then they went and put Him in a grave. Graves in those days were different. They were like small rooms cut out of a rock. There they placed Jesus.

Jesus was in the grave for two days. On the third day, a miracle took place: Jesus woke up! The power of life in God overcame death in the body of Jesus. His heart began beating again. He was raised from the dead. The Lord was alive again. And He still lives!

Be still for a while. Tell the Lord you are very thankful that He is not dead. Praise Him because He lives.

THE STRANGE DONKEY

Then the LORD opened the donkey's mouth,
and she said to Balaam ... (Numbers 22:28)

Balaam was a messenger of the Lord. When the king of Moab wanted to use him to put a curse on the Israelites, God told Balaam that he must not do it. No one is allowed to put a curse on the people of the Lord. The king of Moab offered him a lot of money. But Balaam knew he should not go against God's will.

Balaam had a donkey that was on the road with him. When the donkey refused to walk, Balaam hit the donkey. Suddenly the donkey spoke to Balaam.

But after a while Balaam realized it was an angel talking to him. The angel told Balaam that his path was a dangerous one.

Keep your ears open so that you can hear what the Lord wants to tell you. He even talked to Balaam through a donkey!

THE PRIZE

Run in such a way as to get the prize.
(1 Corinthians 9:24)

Athletes who run a race, run to win a prize. This prize is usually a cup or a trophy or a medal. Basketball, football, or hockey teams can also win a prize. In some sports, like tennis or golf, champions win big money.

We humans will also be rewarded or be given a prize at the end of our lives. There are both winners and losers in life, just like in a race or a match. The Bible says if you don't believe in Jesus and don't want to walk the road of life with Him, you will be a loser one day. You won't get a prize. Only eternal damnation will be waiting for you. On the other hand, everyone who asks Jesus' forgiveness and has been led onto the right road by Him, will get the prize of ever-lasting life.

THE RIGHT OINTMENT

The anointing you received from Him
remains in you. (1 John 2:27)

In the time of the Bible, kings, priests or prophets were anointed with special oil. This oil had a lovely smell, almost like the nicest perfume today. This oil was usually poured onto someone's head as a sign that the person would be able to do his work. The ointment or oil was the sign of the Holy Spirit who would help that person.

When the Holy Spirit came down on Jesus, He was anointed for the work He had to do. The Bible says you and I have also been anointed. When we give our lives to Jesus, the Holy Spirit is like an ointment that gives us what is necessary to do the work of the Lord, just like in the Old Testament.

Thank the Lord that you have also received His Holy Spirit so that you can be used as His anointed one.

A FRIENDLY GREETING

Greet one another with a kiss of love.
(1 Peter 5:14)

In some countries even men greet each other with a kiss. There are cultures where people don't kiss one another on the mouth, but they rub noses. Every country has its own customs, even with kissing.

In the time of the Bible, all people greeted one another with a kiss. It was a sign that they loved and cared for one another.

We don't have to kiss everyone we see, but we must give one another a hearty greeting. It is always nice to be greeted with a smile by a friendly person. The Bible also says that Christians should always greet one another heartily. They must show other Christians that they love them.

Greet everybody you meet today, especially your Christian friends, and be friendly.

COME BACK

Return to the LORD your God, for He is gracious and compassionate, slow to anger and abounding in love. (Joel 2:13)

Sometimes people run away from God. Adam and Eve did. They lived close to God, but then decided to be disobedient. It got so bad that they were chased out of the Garden of Eden. You and I can also run away from God. The Lord calls us to be close to Him, but sometimes we go our own way.

Do you remember the story of the prodigal son? He decided to leave home. He wanted to do his own thing. So he left home and thought he would have the time of his life in a country far away. But he made a mess of his life. He wasted all his money and started going hungry. He realized that he had made a mistake. He decided to return home. The safest and best place to be is close to God. Tell Him you are sorry. He is waiting for you.

SOW AND REAP

Do not be deceived: God cannot be mocked.
A man reaps what he sows. (Galatians 6:7)

Everything you and I do has consequences. If we put our hand on a hot stove, we will be burned. If we drive into a wall, we will get hurt. If we keep on watching ugly things on TV, we will become ugly in our hearts. There are also positive consequences of what we do. If you have studied hard you will probably get good grades. If you treat others well, they will do the same to you. When you serve the Lord, your love for Him grows.

The Bible says what you sow, you will reap. The fruit in our lives depends on the good or bad seed we sowed. If you think bad things, you will do bad things.

See that you do what is good and right according to God's will.

WHOM ARE YOU INVITING?

Philip found Nathanael and told him ... "Come and see." (John 1:45, 46)

There once was a man called Philip. He had a friend named Nathanael.

Philip met Jesus one day. He saw Him and heard what He had to say. While he was listening to Jesus, he was sure that Jesus was the Redeemer that God had sent. The more he listened, the more he realized the truth of this. When Philip saw Nathanael, he was very excited and told him about Jesus – that he was the one Moses wrote about in the Law and the one about whom the prophets had spoken. Nathanael was not impressed. He could not believe that this Jesus could be so important. But Philip invited Nathanael to come and see for himself. A miracle took place. Jesus talked to Nathanael, and he realized that Jesus was the Son of God.

Do you tell people about Jesus?

ONLY TWO ROADS

"Wide is the gate and broad is the road that leads to destruction ... but small is the gate and narrow the road that leads to life." (Matthew 7:13, 14)

The Bible tells us there are only two roads to choose between. One is a broad road. There are many people on this road. Unfortunately, this road leads to a very bad place. The Bible calls it the place of destruction. We also call it hell.

Fortunately, there is also another road. This is a narrow road. Not many people take this road. Although few people walk on this road, they know they are on the right road if they do. The Lord walks this road with them. This is the road to life, or heaven.

You must choose which road you want to take. God calls us to choose the narrow road. On this road we ask what the Lord's will is and then we live according to it.

ON THE ROAD WITH JESUS

"Were not our hearts burning within us while He talked with us on the road and opened the Scriptures to us?" (Luke 24:32)

After Jesus' resurrection, two of His disciples were on the road to Emmaus. As they talked, Jesus came up to them and started interpreting the Scriptures for them. This means He taught them about the things written in the Word of God. While they were on the way, they learned what the Lord's will was, especially about His death and resurrection. Later on He ate with them, and only then did they realize it was Jesus. Then He suddenly disappeared.

Something you cannot explain happens to you when the Lord speaks to your heart. You get a feeling of peace and joy. It is a warm feeling.

Go on the road with Jesus today. Allow Him to explain His Word to you.

CELEBRATING YOUR FREEDOM

"So if the Son sets you free, you will be free indeed." (John 8:36)

Many countries have special days on which they celebrate the freedom which they enjoy. It is wonderful to live in a land of liberty where individual rights and choices are honored and protected.

The Bible, however, says that you are not free simply because you live in a free country. Even if there is not war or a conflict in a country, there can be many bonds that bind people. It does not have to be political bonds; bonds of hatred and bad relationships between people are just as real.

Jesus said very clearly that a person is never really free if he is not free from sin.

Spread this message of freedom: Jesus is the Person who brings true liberty and freedom.

WHO ARE YOUR FRIENDS?

Oh, the joys of those who do not follow the advice of the wicked, or stand around with sinners, or join in with mockers.
(Psalm 1:1, NLT)

Although we are children of this world, we are not to live like worldly children. We chose to follow Jesus, and that is why we try to do what the Lord tells us to.

Today's Scripture verse says we will be blessed if we choose our friends well. A Christian is friendly to all people, whether they know the Lord or not. But a Christian cannot become close friends with just anybody. Our best friends must be friends who also know the Lord and love Him.

It would be better to choose friends from those who follow the counsel of the Lord and want to think like Him, those who have been washed clean of their sins. Who are your best friends?

PRAY FOR PEACE

Why do the nations conspire and the peoples plot in vain? (Psalm 2:1)

All over the world there is unrest and strife. Every day we see on TV or read in the papers about warring countries. People kill one another, and we hear of uprisings and dissatisfaction. Many children go hungry or get hurt and die because they are caught up in a war where they live.

Psalm 2 tells us that the real reason for all the wars and strife in the world is because kings and presidents and the leaders of countries do not want to bow to God and accept His rule.

Jesus came to build a kingdom of peace. He promised that if we follow Him we will live in peace. If countries and their leaders will accept the kingship of Jesus, there will be peace.

Let us pray for our country and our leaders.

LIFT UP MY HEAD

You bestow glory on me and lift up my head. (Psalm 3:3)

What God thinks of you and me is most important. It is also important what others think of us. Every one of us has an opinion of another human being. Opinions differ and are often wrong, yet it is important what people think of us.

Sometimes people change their opinion of us. If we do good, someone might think we are not as bad as they thought. If we do wrong, someone's opinion of us can also change.

It is important that the Lord's opinion of us must be correct. We all make mistakes and all of us sometimes do things that are not right. If we tell the Lord that we are sorry, He forgives us. His opinion doesn't change. He knows we are sinful, but He sees we are feeling bad about it, and that is enough for Him.

MY HEART IS OVERFLOWING

You have filled my heart with greater joy than when ... grain and new wine abound.
(Psalm 4:7)

We all make the mistake of thinking if we have possessions we will be happy. Some think if they get a bigger house they will be happy. Others think if they can drive a better car they will be happy. Perhaps you think if you can get a new bicycle you will be happy. Or a nice watch, or a lovely dress, or that special something you so badly want.

David was a king and he had many possessions. Still he wrote these words to tell you and me that he has learned that many possessions do not really make one happy. It is not what you have, but what you have in your heart that makes you happy.

David's heart was overflowing with the joy of the Lord.

SCARED OF THE NIGHT

I will lie down and sleep in peace, for You alone, O LORD, make me dwell in safety. (Psalm 4:8)

We live in a very unsafe world. Every day we hear about people who are attacked and shot even in their own homes. This is enough to scare anyone. Bad people often use the dark of the night to commit their crimes.

David, as a king, had many worries. One day his son Absalom did something very bad. It was so bad that David had to flee for his life. Yet we hear him say that he will lie down and sleep in peace. This tells us that David had complete trust in the Lord. He believed that God alone could protect him. He slept peacefully.

God is with us. He never slumbers or sleeps. He will look after us.

THE NEW MORNING

In the morning, O LORD, You hear my voice;
in the morning I lay my requests before You
and wait in expectation. (Psalm 5:3)

In the morning when we get up, there is usually lots to do. Some of us must make our beds. We must eat breakfast and get ready for the day. We must brush our teeth and make sure that our hair is combed neatly.

As soon as possible after we have woken up we should speak to the Lord. As soon as you are awake, say, "Good morning, Lord." Ask Him to be with you all day long. If you have a moment later on, read a few verses of Scripture; see what He says and pray for specific things. The Lord listens to your voice in the morning.

If we pray, we will receive. Talk to the Lord now.

HEAL ME, LORD

O LORD, heal me, for my bones are in agony.
(Psalm 6:2)

There are many millions of people in the world who are sick today. Maybe you are also sick. It's not nice to be ill, because then you can't play and have fun.

Fortunately, we as Christians can ask the Lord to help us when we are ill. David did. He asked the Lord to please make him well. The Lord helps us in all our troubles.

Ask the Lord in faith to heal you. If you are not ill, think of someone you know who is ill. Pray for them now, or write a card and say you are thinking of them. Thank the Lord for your health.

IT'S NOT FAIR

God is a righteous judge. (Psalm 7:11)

People are often treated unfairly. It means that you get what you did not deserve. Someone else did something wrong and now you get blamed. Someone else was bad and now you are scolded!

Sometimes you and I can say we didn't do it because we were not guilty. There are other times we cannot even do that. We just hear that someone blamed us behind our backs for something we didn't do. It is impossible for us to defend ourselves. Then it is better to let it go and accept that there is nothing you can do!

Luckily there is a fair judge: the Lord. He knows what goes on in your heart. He can be trusted. If you are treated unfairly today, give the matter to God. Just make sure you live the way you should and do what He tells you.

SING A NEW SONG

Sing to the LORD a new song; sing to the LORD all the earth. (Psalm 96:1)

The Bible says in a few places that we must sing a new song to the Lord. Does this mean that we must look for songs that we have never heard? That we must sing only fresh, new songs?

The Bible says that old songs are songs sung in the hearts and thoughts of people still living with sin. Sin always makes things feel old. Sin often looks fresh and new, but very soon you find out that this is not true. Sin brings unhappiness. Jesus, on the other hand, gives us new life.

A broken guitar or a broken violin cannot play beautiful music. Only when you fix it can you play fresh, new music. In the same way the Lord fixes us when we have sinned. Everything in our lives and in our hearts that praises the Lord – that is what the Bible calls a new song.

TIME IS PRECIOUS

Make the most of every opportunity.
(Colossians 4:5)

Time is like a stream. The water flows past, and when each drop of water has flowed past, it will never come that way again. It is the same with our time. We have an opportunity to do things today. If we don't do them, we might never be able to do them again. Today's time we cannot have over again tomorrow.

It is important to the Lord that we use every opportunity to live for Him. Every second is precious. Every minute is important. Every hour that we can live for Him is valuable. We must know that every day could be our last. Every month gives us the opportunity to tell others about Him and to live for Him. Every year is a precious opportunity to learn more about the Lord.

Thank the Lord for this day. Make the best of it!

EMBRACE HIM

Exalt the LORD our God. (Psalm 99:5)

To praise the Lord is wonderful. When we praise Him, we sing merry, joyful songs that say the Lord is great and wonderful. Songs of praise are full of joy. We sing to say that we are excited because the Lord is wonderful.

Christians don't sing only songs of praise, but also songs to worship. Worshiping the Lord is a little different from praising Him. The Bible uses a word for worship that means something like "to come closer, to embrace."

We cannot embrace God like a human. He is not in a body here with us. But we can love the Lord with our hearts and in our thoughts. We can tell Him of our love and feel it deep in our hearts. We can also sing Him songs of worship. Come, let's worship Him right now.

LIKE GRASS

Our days on earth are like grass. The wind blows, and we are gone.
(Psalm 103:15-16, NLT)

Some people reach the age of ninety. Others forty. Then there are those who die very young. Our lives are transient. This means that nothing lasts forever, it comes to an end. I'm sure you have flowers in your garden. Today you see a beautiful flower, but tomorrow or the next day the flower has wilted and has died. You will never see that flower again. It is the same with a human life. We don't live on earth forever. People who may be fit and strong today, could be dead tomorrow.

Only people who accept the new life Jesus gives, will live forever. Are you glad that you will live forever with Jesus in heaven?

THE SPECIAL STONE

The stone the builders rejected has become the cornerstone. (Psalm 118:22)

One day some people wanted to erect a building. They built with stone. Among all the other stones was a very special stone. This special stone looked quite ordinary to them, so they took this stone and threw it to one side. God, however, knew that this was a special stone. He used it as the most important stone in His building. He made it the cornerstone or foundation of the building.

This is just a story, but this is what happened to Jesus. When Jesus came to earth, the Pharisees and scribes thought that He was just an ordinary person. But Jesus was very special. God used Jesus as a cornerstone to build the new Jerusalem, where all the children of God will live together happily.

CALL OUT TO GOD

I call on the LORD in my distress, and He answers me. (Psalm 120:1)

Have you ever been in big trouble? It could be that you lost something very valuable. At that moment when you realized it, your heart missed a beat.

The Bible says a child of the Lord calls out to God in a moment of crisis. It is the right thing to do. You can even start praying out loud when you realize you are in trouble. Don't be ashamed to do it. Call out to God; He is there with you. It will be good for everyone, including the devil, to hear that you put your trust in the Lord. Calling on the name of the Lord, is like running to hide safely in a strong tower.

Remember that you can always call upon the Lord in your distress.

THE TEARS WERE FLOWING

By the rivers of Babylon we sat and wept when we remembered Zion. (Psalm 137:1)

Israel did evil in the eyes of the Lord. Therefore God allowed them to be exiled to Babylon. The Babylonians were a heathen nation. They did not believe in God. The Israelites found it very difficult to live in a foreign country.

Someone then wrote a song that tells how they sat at the rivers of Babylon and cried because they missed Zion, the mountain on which the beautiful city of Jerusalem stood.

If you are not prepared to do the will of the Lord, you cannot really be happy. If you drag your sins along with you, you will always reach a point where the happiness and joy in your heart disappear. Sin always brings unhappiness. You and I cannot sing in our hearts and be joyful if we sin.

A PARENT'S ADVICE

Listen, my sons, to a father's instruction;
pay attention and gain understanding.
(Proverbs 4:1)

Parents must teach their children and advise them. When fathers and mothers don't really love their children, then it's not important to them what their children do. Parents who care about them, teach their children well. It is good when parents teach their children right from wrong.

Children, on the other hand, don't always take the advice of their parents to heart. It is a foolish child who does not want to accept advice from his or her parents. We do not always like getting advice from older people because we think what we want to do is better. Accept that grown-ups have more experience, and that is why their advice is good.

Thank the Lord for your parents today.

LIKE THE RISING SUN

"May they who love You be like the sun when it rises in its strength." (Judges 5:31)

Especially in winter, it is lovely when the sun shines brightly. Sun brings warmth. When you open the curtains in a cold house, the room quickly becomes nice and warm. When we sit in the winter sun, our bodies warm up.

The Bible says whoever loves the Lord can shine brightly like the rising sun. Their lives, the way they act, their friendliness and love, can be like bright sunshine on a cold winter's day. You and I can, as children of the Lord, bring light and warmth wherever we go. Jesus said we must be the light of the world. Jesus Himself is called the light of the world. If He, the brightest light, lives in us, our lives are also lit up, and we will shine like bright sunbeams in the dark.

Bring sunshine today wherever you go.

ENOUGH

"Even if she gathers among the sheaves, don't embarrass her." (Ruth 2:15)

After Naomi's husband and sons died, she wanted to go back to Bethlehem. Ruth, her daughter-in-law decided to go with her.

In Bethlehem they had to find food to eat. Ruth went to the fields where they were harvesting the wheat. As the men were gathering the sheaves, some leftover grain remained in the fields. In those times poor people were allowed to gather behind the harvesters. This cornfield belonged to Boaz. He was a good man. He saw how hard Ruth was working and he told his men to leave more grain behind so that she could gather more. It was the Lord working in Boaz's heart. Later Boaz married Ruth.

The Lord looks after His children. Ruth worked hard, and the Lord blessed her. The Lord wants to take care of you too.

GOOD LEADERS

In those days Israel had no king; everyone did as he saw fit. (Judges 21:25)

In Judges 21 we read how the young men from Benjamin (the Benjamites) hid in the vineyards, and when the young girls from the town of Shiloh came out to dance in the field, they rushed out, and each one grabbed himself a wife. What a way to get a wife! I don't think the Lord was very happy with this because the chapter closes saying that at the time there was no king, and everyone did as they pleased. If all of us do what we please, life will be very confusing. Just think: if everyone drives a car as fast as they like, there will be a lot more accidents on the roads.

It is important to have leaders. Leaders are people who are chosen or appointed to see that rules are obeyed. It is your duty to keep to the rules and obey leaders.

ANSWERED PRAYER

She named him Samuel, saying, "Because I asked the LORD for him." (1 Samuel 1:20)

There was a woman called Hannah in the Bible. Her husband's name was Elkanah. He loved Hannah very much. But Hannah was very sad because she could not have a baby. She wanted a baby badly, but she and her husband had no children. Then Hannah went to the temple. Hannah pleaded with God and begged that He would work a miracle. She also made the Lord a promise. She said if she had a child, she would give this child to the Lord. The Lord answered Hannah's prayer. A miracle happened! Suddenly she was expecting a baby. His name was Samuel. When Samuel was big enough, she took him to the temple, and there he worked for the Lord.

Remember, if you make a promise to the Lord, you must keep it.

THE RIGHT FRIENDS

When Saul returned to his home at Gibeah, a group of men whose hearts God had touched went with him.
(1 Samuel 10:26, NLT)

The people of Israel wanted a king. So the Lord gave them a king, but He warned them that kings can make life difficult. The first king was Saul. Saul was just an ordinary young man. Suddenly he was a king. He must have felt a bit lonely and also unsure of how he should behave.

Then God made a plan. He "touched" the hearts of a number of brave men. This means that the Lord put it into their hearts that they should support Saul.

God knows that we can sometimes not do what we have to do when we are alone. Then He touches the hearts of friends to love and support us. Pray that the Lord will send you the right friends.

GOD'S ANSWERS

But God did not answer him that day.
(1 Samuel 14:37)

We know that we can't hear the voice of the Lord the way we can another person's. God talks in different ways. He speaks to us through the Holy Spirit and through His Word. Sometimes He speaks through people, but what they say will never go against God's Word.

If you have prayed about a thing and have asked the Lord to give you wisdom, He will sometimes give you an answer deep inside your heart. You just know what His will is. Then there are times when you ask and ask and get no reply. It is as if the Lord is keeping quiet. That may be because you are asking things that go against His will.

Trust that the Lord knows best. If what you have asked for is really meant for you, He will give it to you, at the right time.

GOD SEES INSIDE

"The LORD doesn't see things the way you see them. People judge by outward appearance, but the LORD looks at the heart."
(1 Samuel 16:7)

King Saul disappointed the Lord, and so the Lord decided to choose a new king. Samuel was the prophet who had to anoint the new king. He didn't know whom he had to anoint. All he knew was that it would be one of the sons of Jesse.

Jesse had eight sons. They were good-looking, big, and strong. Samuel thought the biggest and strongest and most attractive son would become the new king. But God wanted someone who was attractive in his heart. The Lord chose David. He was the youngest, and not the strongest or the best looking. When Samuel saw David, the Lord spoke in Samuel's heart and told him that this was the new king that he had to anoint.

PEACE IN MUSIC

Whenever the tormenting spirit from God troubled Saul, David would play the harp. Then Saul would feel better, and the tormenting spirit would go away.
(1 Samuel 16:23, NLT)

B ecause Saul sinned, the Lord allowed an evil spirit to trouble him and make him unhappy.

David played the harp beautifully. The harp in those days was a stringed instrument, nearly like a guitar. David learned to play the harp when he looked after his father's sheep in the fields. That is where he sang many of the psalms that we can still read in the Bible today. Saul often asked David to play him some music, especially when Saul's heart was troubled. Whenever David began playing, Saul would have peace in his heart again. Songs or music sung or played by Christians help to bring Christ's light and peace into the world.

SOMEONE ELSE

"He is the one who will build a house for My Name." (2 Samuel 7:13)

Ki ng David loved the Lord. He was a successful king and very famous. The Israelites prospered when he was king.

Still, there was something David wanted to do very badly: he wanted to build a house for the Lord. In the Old Testament times, they had to go to a building or tent that was set aside for talking to the Lord or worshiping Him. David wanted to build a big and beautiful temple for the Lord. He dreamed about it and planned to build this place for God.

But the Lord had His own plan. He wanted David's son to build this temple. The prophet Nathan came to tell David this. Sometimes you and I also want to do something badly, but the Lord wants to use someone else. We may be disappointed, but the Lord knows best.

AN EVIL PLAN

*He got up and went down to take posses-
sion of Naboth's vineyard. (1 Kings 21:16)*

King Ahab was a bad man who married a
wicked woman, Jezebel.

Ahab had enough money and possessions. But he was not satisfied. He saw a
very nice vineyard. It belonged to Naboth.
He told Naboth that he wanted to buy
the vineyard. Naboth did not want to sell
it because he had inherited the ground. It
was special to him. Then King Ahab started
sulking. His bad wife told him what to do;
it was an evil plan. Ahab arranged for two
men to lie about Naboth. They accused
him of doing things that he had not done.
Ahab ordered that Naboth had to be
stoned to death. After Naboth's death the
king took Naboth's vineyard for himself.

Don't ever hurt someone just because
you want something that belongs to him.

YOU WILL BE COMFORTED

"As a mother comforts her child, so will I comfort you." (Isaiah 66:13)

If you pick up a baby unexpectedly or put him in the arms of a stranger, he will usually start crying. This happens because the baby does not feel safe.

You and I also have things that make us feel insecure and afraid. The Lord does not want us to feel insecure. When a child feels insecure, he or she usually runs to Mommy, where there is safety. Mothers and fathers protect their children and take them in their arms so that they can feel there is no danger. As a mother comforts her child, the Lord will also comfort you and me.

We must just trust Him, run to Him, and shelter with Him. He will put His arms around us and we will feel safe.

THREE IMPORTANT THINGS

"I will bless those who have humble and contrite hearts, who tremble at My word." (Isaiah 66:2, NLT)

When the Lord looks at a person, there are certain things that are important to Him. If He finds these qualities in a person, He is like a father who looks at His child with satisfaction and love. The first thing of importance is that we must not be proud. We must realize our need and ask help. If we do, we can be helped. A proud person will not admit that he needs help. That is why the Lord cannot help a proud person.

The second thing is to repent of our sins. If you don't say you are sorry you cannot be forgiven. If you confess your sins, God will forgive you. The third important thing the Lord likes very much is when His words are important to us. He likes people who respect His words.

A BROKEN JUG

... broken cisterns that cannot hold water.
(Jeremiah 2:13)

In biblical times, people didn't have taps in their homes that they could just turn on to get water. They had to go to a well, or another source of water, and carry it home in a stone jug or a pail.

A jug or a pail can hold water only if it does not have holes in it. Otherwise it will leak. One day the Lord told Jeremiah that His followers were just like people trying to draw water with a jug that has a hole in it. The more water they drew, the less water they had, because they kept on losing the water. The Lord used this image to show that people did not put their trust in Him, but in ordinary people with shortcomings.

We must trust God. He will never disappoint us like a broken jug.

GOD'S SAD HEART

My heart is faint within me. Listen to the
cry of my people from a land far away.
(Jeremiah 8:18, 19)

Have you ever wondered if God can be sad? We read in the Bible that the Lord was very sad when He looked at the people of Israel. He wanted only the best for them, but they sinned. Then He looked at them and saw how they were suffering. What the Lord saw made Him sad and upset. He saw how troubled they were in their distress. Then He said, "Since My people are crushed, I am crushed; I mourn, and horror grips Me" (verse 21).

The Lord so badly wants to comfort His people, to be like an ointment that will heal the wounds of their hurt. He wishes they will accept Him and come back to Him. Only He can help them.

Come to the Lord today so that His heart can be filled with joy.

BE CAREFUL OF BOASTING

But let him who boasts boast about this that he understands and knows Me.
(Jeremiah 9:24)

When we can do something well, it is easy to boast. When we boast, we tell others how good we are at certain things. Some people sing beautifully, others run fast or are smart. Often our fathers and mothers or grandmothers and grandfathers boast about us.

The Lord said a wise man must not boast about his wisdom. The soldier must not boast about his great strength. A rich man must not boast about his great wealth. If we have to boast, there is only one thing to boast about, and that is the Lord Himself.

Someone who is wise never boasts about himself, but he says the Lord is good and wonderful. He is the one who gives us our talents. He must take credit for it.

WHEN ALL IS WELL ...

Give glory to the LORD your God before ... your feet stumble on the darkening hills. (Jeremiah 13:16)

Most people call out to God only when things go wrong. Every day they just go on living their lives, and when something goes wrong, they call upon the Lord. Then they think He must help quickly. The Lord wants us to put our trust in Him, and He wants to help people in need. But He does not like it if we ask His help just when we are in trouble.

The Lord says His people must glorify Him before it gets dark in their lives. In the dark we can't see where we are going, and the Lord uses this image to say, "They will be like people who bump into the mountain in the dark." We must not wait until the moment of need. Speak to the Lord now, and glorify and praise Him for everything He is and does.

HE IS EVERYWHERE

"Do not I fill heaven and earth?" declares the LORD. (Jeremiah 23:24)

There are really people who think they can hide from the Lord. The Lord says no one can "hide in secret places so that I cannot see him" (verse 24). God sees everything because He is everywhere. He can see deep into our hearts. Yes, God knows everything and sees everything.

It scares some people to think that God knows everything about them and can see everything. If you are the Lord's child, it doesn't scare you; it makes you happy. It means that the Lord understands you. He knows what you are struggling with. He knows what your problems are. He also knows what your dreams are and what you want or need.

Thank the Lord that He knows all about you and sees everything you do – and that He still loves you very much.

THE FIRE AND THE HAMMER

"Is not My word like fire," declares the LORD, "and like a hammer that breaks a rock in pieces?" (Jeremiah 23:29)

The Bible is very, very powerful. Many people have read the Bible just because they were inquisitive, and then their whole lives were changed. There are many people who have spent the night in a hotel room where a Bible was placed next to the bed, and when they started reading it, it was as if their attention was fixed on it, and they could not put it down. Suddenly they realized that God was talking to them, and they made their peace with God.

Small wonder that the Bible says that God's Word is like fire. It can change a person's life.

The Bible is also like a hammer sometimes. You can use it to drive nails in, but you can also use it to break down walls. The Word can change your life.

THE PAST IS PAST

"Do not dwell on the past. See I am doing a new thing!" (Isaiah 43:18, 19)

We can all remember something that happened in the past. Perhaps it was something good, or maybe something bad. You must not allow the ugly things of the past to spoil today's joy. The Lord prefers that we live each day to the full, one day at a time.

We know that the Lord is the One who wants to make the good things in our lives even better. That is why He says we must not think too much about past things, because He is going to do something new, and it is about to happen. God also makes another promise. Even if tomorrow is a desert, He will give us enough water.

Leave all the hurt of the past in His hands, and trust Him to give you a new, bright future.

THE HOUSE COLLAPSED

"The winds blew and beat against that house, and it fell with a great crash."
(Matthew 7:27)

The Lord told many parables. A parable is a story with a message. The parable that Jesus is telling here is about a man who built a house. But this house he built on sand. The storms and the rain came with lightning and thunder, and the house collapsed completely.

Another man built a house. He made sure that his house was not built on sand, but on a firm foundation (a rock). The lesson of this parable is that every person's life, yours too, is like a house. There are many storms in this world that can hurt us and destroy our lives. But if we build on the right Foundation, that is Jesus Christ, then the house or our life will remain standing in the face of all the storms of life.

MUSICIANS

Four thousand are to praise the LORD with the musical instruments I have provided for that purpose. (1 Chronicles 23:5)

Today there are many musicians and singers who are used by the Lord to glorify and praise Him. Many congregations have members who sing beautifully, and they lead the congregation in praising the Lord. The message that they sing is the message of the wonderful gospel of Jesus.

In the time of the Old Testament, singers and musicians were appointed, and it was their full-time job to help people praise and glorify the Lord. King David was a musician himself. In his time he appointed thousands of singers and paid them all a salary to praise the Lord.

Thank the Lord for singers and musicians who help us to praise and love the Lord better.

JOSHUA'S FILTHY CLOTHES

Now Joshua [the high priest] was dressed in filthy clothes. (Zechariah 3:3)

Zechariah was one of the Lord's prophets. One day he saw a vision, which was like a dream. The Lord often talked to His prophets in dreams. In these dreams the Lord tried to tell them something He wanted them to know.

Zechariah's dream was about the priest called Joshua who did very important work. He was the high priest. Next to Joshua stood the devil. He was busy accusing Joshua. But the Lord scolded Satan because He still had a plan for Joshua. Joshua's clothes were filthy with sin. The Lord told an angel to take off his dirty clothes. Then the Lord said to Joshua, "See, I have taken away your sin, and I will put rich garments [clean clothes] on you" (verse 4).

Pray for your minister so that he can be clean when he stands before the Lord.

GOOD COMPANY

"Bad company corrupts good character."
(1 Corinthians 15:33)

It is always interesting to see how people react when they are in the company of different people.

Our behavior is influenced by the company we keep. You can talk softly, but the minute someone starts shouting at you, it is not long before you shout right back at them. When someone is ticking you off and you speak softly, it is interesting that the noisy person quickly starts talking softly.

This is the way we influence one another. The company you keep is important. If you are always in the company of people who say and do ugly things, you eventually become just like them. That is why the Bible tells us we must be careful of the company we keep. Make sure you keep the right company today so that your behavior will be to the glory of God.

GIFTS FROM GOD

There are different kinds of gifts, but the same Spirit. (1 Corinthians 12:4)

It is always exciting to receive gifts. If you are a child of the Lord, you also receive gifts. The gifts the Lord gives you are handed out by the Holy Spirit who lives in a Christian. The Bible calls these gifts "gifts of grace." "Grace" means that these gifts are free; you and I just get them, not because we deserve them. "Gift" means just that – it is a present. So gifts of grace are gifts we haven't earned; we get them free from the hand of God.

These are gifts to share with others. Every Christian has received a gift from God. This gift is something like wisdom, knowledge, special faith, or even the ability to bring God's healing to others. The Holy Spirit hands out these gifts to the children of God. We must ask God to show us which gift He gave us.

PRAY FOR YOUR COUNTRY

Righteousness exalts a nation, but sin is a disgrace to any people. (Proverbs 14:34)

We live in God's beautiful world. Each country is unique and known for specific things. South Africa for example is a country of sunshine, and friendly people.

Unfortunately there are things in any country that are not at all beautiful. Terrible things happen, and people do evil things. They don't know the Lord and do not love Him. They are people who sin. Sin always brings shame on a country and its people.

The Lord says that when we pray He will answer our prayers and help us. Why don't you and I ask the Lord's forgiveness for all our sins, also on behalf of our country. We must say, "Lord, we are sorry that not all of us want to serve You. Forgive us, help us, and heal our country. Grant that we can live here in safety, and in peace."

NOT NICE ANYMORE

Better a meal of vegetables where there is love than a fattened calf with hatred.
(Proverbs 15:17)

You can have the most delicious food at mealtime: fried potatoes and a big steak, with ice cream, or other sorts of goodies. But if the atmosphere at the table is not pleasant, then the food does not taste as good as it should. Perhaps it has happened that you were enjoying a good meal, when all of a sudden some argument started. That's when we get angry with one another and say mean things to each other. I bet the food was suddenly not as nice anymore.

A wise man wrote in the Bible that he would rather eat plain vegetables served with love, than a delicious, exotic meal served with hatred.

Every day you when say grace before a meal, pray that the love and peace of the Lord be there with you all.

BROTHERS AND SISTERS

He said, "Here are My mother and My brothers. For whoever does the will of My Father in heaven is My brother and sister and mother." (Matthew 12:49, 50)

To have family is wonderful. The members of a family can help, protect, and love one another. Normally, family members are supposed to give warmth and love to one another, like a harbor where boats can dock safely.

Christian families are not only brothers and sisters living in the same house. Jesus surprised people when He said He did not have only one mother and a few brothers. He said that everyone who does the will of His Father is a brother or a sister to Him.

Christians must love one another like brothers and sisters. We must care for one another, support one another, and encourage one another to serve the Lord.

DO IT NOW

Do not say to your neighbor, "Come back later; I'll give it tomorrow." (Proverbs 3:28)

It always feels good to help others. But when you are asked to help out, it isn't always easy to turn your attention to them immediately. Also, it might not be so easy or pleasant while you are busy helping them. But when you have helped them, you have a good feeling inside. It is good when people help one another.

Sometimes we are so busy that we do not think it will be possible to help the person asking for it now. Then we say, "I can't do it right now, Mom." The Bible says we shouldn't do that. When someone asks us, we must do it immediately.

If we are asked to help, do it now.

PUNISHMENT IS PAINFUL

Those who spare the rod of discipline hate their children. Those who love their children care enough to discipline them.
(Proverbs 13:24, NLT)

Parents punish their children because they want to teach them right from wrong. The government punishes people who break the law. The Lord punishes people who break His laws. Punishment is part of our lives. Sometimes we think our parents don't love us when they discipline us. No parent or teacher or anyone else may punish someone without a good reason. If, however, we deserve to be punished, it will make us think twice the next time we want to do something wrong.

Because your parents love you, they punish you by taking something away from you, or making you stay in your room for a while. If you have been punished, apologize, and try not to do the same thing again.

THE PRECIOUS PEARL

"When he found a pearl of great value, he went away and sold everything he had and bought it." (Matthew 13:46)

Jesus told stories to teach people important things. He told the story of a man who worked with jewels. He was always on the lookout for good pearls to string and sell, and he made a lot of money like this.

This jeweler came across a very wonderful pearl one day. It was the best pearl he had ever seen. He knew immediately that it was very valuable. So he went and sold all his goods so that he could buy this most important, most valuable pearl.

Jesus told this story to tell us that His kingdom is just as important as the most valuable pearl. There is nothing more important than to know the Lord, to serve Him as your king, and be His follower in this kingdom.

SEED BECOMES A TREE

"Though it is the smallest of your seeds, yet when it grows, it is the largest of garden plants and becomes a tree." (Matthew 13:32)

The seed of the mustard plant is so small that you can hardly see it. But this little seed can become a big tree.

One can hardly believe that some big trees grow from a small seed. A small mustard seed also grows into a tall tree, and many birds build their nests in the branches of that tree. This is the image the Lord used to say that His kingdom will be like that. Just think of this: Jesus began, as one Person on earth, to tell people about His kingdom, and today millions of people are part of this kingdom.

This is how Christians build the kingdom. We carry the seed of the Word, and it grows in our hearts; we give some to others so that the seed can also come up in their hearts.

ON THE WATER

But when Peter saw the wind, he was afraid and, beginning to sink, cried out, "Lord, save me!" (Matthew 14:30)

One day the disciples were all in a boat a few miles from the shore. Suddenly the wind started blowing, and it whipped up great waves on the Sea of Galilee. The disciples were on this stormy sea all night.

At daybreak, Jesus came walking toward them on the sea. The disciples were afraid because they thought it was a ghost. Jesus said to them, "Don't be afraid, it is I." Peter could not believe it was Jesus. He said, "Jesus, if this is really You, tell me to walk on the water to You."

Peter began walking on the water, but when he saw how big the waves were, he was afraid and started sinking.

We must trust in the Lord completely.

THE LONE SHEEP

"Will he not leave the ninety-nine ... and go to look for the one that wandered off?"
(Matthew 18:12)

Jesus told the parable of a man who had one hundred sheep. Every day he left them to graze in the fields.

One sheep wanted more green grass and went after it. This sheep strayed from the others. All of a sudden he was alone and couldn't see the other sheep anywhere.

Because the shepherd knew all his sheep, he soon noticed that one sheep was missing. He left the ninety-nine others together and went looking for the lost sheep. When he found him, he was so happy that he held him close.

You and I must go and look for lost people and point them back to Jesus. They are very important to Him.

WHAT GOD EXPECTS

"Love the Lord your God with all your heart ... Love your neighbor as yourself."
(Matthew 22:37, 39)

If we should ask what the Lord really expects from you and me, we would be able to give two answers from the Bible.

The first important thing is that we must love the Lord our God with all our heart and all our soul and all our mind. We must choose God. We must tell Him that we love Him. We must want to live for Him. This is the first and greatest commandment.

The second thing the Lord wants from us is that we must love not only Him but also all people around us. We must show them the love of the Lord.

Love for the Lord and love for people – this is what the Lord wants to see. Love God today and also everyone you meet.

PREPARING THE WAY

"A voice ... calling in the desert, 'Prepare the way for the Lord, make straight paths for Him ... And all mankind will see God's salvation.'" (Luke 3:4, 6)

Already in Isaiah it was prophesied that someone would do the work to prepare the way for the Lord.

Before Jesus started telling people about His kingdom, John the Baptist (who was a relative of His) was already preaching in the desert near the Jordan River. He told people to repent. He also told them that someone was coming who would bring salvation. In this way he prepared the way for Jesus. He told people that Jesus would come with a plan for salvation.

You and I must also try to make it easier for Jesus to reach people with the gospel of salvation. Like John we must say, "Make straight paths for Him" so that people can be prepared for Him.

USELESS LAMPS

"Give us some of your oil." (Matthew 25:8)

Jesus told the parable of ten girls who took their lamps to meet a bridegroom. In Jesus' time wedding celebrations lasted much longer than they do today. Because it was getting dark they needed lamps. Five of the girls didn't take extra oil with them. The bridegroom was late, and their lamps started going out. They asked the other girls for oil, but there was not enough for everyone and they had to go and buy oil. While they were gone, the bridegroom arrived, and everyone who was there went with him. When the girls whose lamps had gone out came back, the bridegroom and his guests had already left.

This parable means that you and I must always be prepared so that when Jesus comes back again as He promised, we will be ready to go with Him.

PERFUME FOR JESUS

*A woman came to Him with an alabaster
jar of very expensive perfume, which she
poured on His head. (Matthew 26:7)*

In the days when Jesus was on earth,
people liked sweet-smelling stuff. After all,
they could not shower as frequently as we
can. Instead, they used perfumed oil. This
oil was very expensive.

One day when Jesus was in Bethany,
in the home of Simon, a woman came to
Him where He was sitting at the table and
poured a very expensive jar of oil on His
head. It was a wonderful thing to do. Jesus
was very thankful and pleased with what
the woman had done. One of Jesus' disciples
was angry because so much money was
wasted on Jesus' hair, but Jesus knew that
this woman was glorifying Him.

We honor Jesus when we praise Him,
give our lives to Him, follow Him, and just
tell Him that we love Him.

ARE YOU HOSPITABLE?

Practice hospitality. (Romans 12:13)

It is always nice to visit hospitable people. Hospitable people have open hearts for visitors. Anyone who walks through their door instantly feels welcome. There is an atmosphere of warmth and friendliness. It almost feels as if you are at home.

Hospitality is a very good characteristic. If you open up your heart and home to others, they enjoy being with you.

The Lord likes us to be hospitable. He likes it when we show others that we love them. We show our love when we make others feel at home. We make them a nice cup of tea or coffee, and we offer them food if they are hungry. If they want to sleep over, we give them a warm bed.

Think of ways you can be hospitable to others today.

GOD HAS A PLAN

The king had granted him everything he asked, for the hand of the LORD his God was on him. (Ezra 7:6)

The people of Israel were exiled to Persia because they did not do the will of the Lord. Ezra was one of the Israelites who lived in Babylon, in Persia. God had a plan for Ezra.

The Lord decided that His people had lived in a foreign country long enough. It was time for them to go back to Israel. He wanted the temple to be rebuilt. Ezra was one of the important people He wanted to use for this purpose. The Lord kept His hand on Ezra in a special way, and he found favor with the king of Persia, Artaxerxes.

If you serve the Lord, He will even use non-Christians to favor you so that you can finish your work.

EZRA'S EXAMPLE

For Ezra had devoted himself to the study ...
of the Law of the LORD, and to teaching its
decrees and laws in Israel. (Ezra 7:10)

O ften people ask us what we are going to do during the holidays or what we want to do when we have finished school. We all have a dream or an ideal. What is your ideal? Ezra had a specific task. The Bible says he devoted himself to do certain things. "Devoted" means we do something with enthusiasm and faith. If you want to see or do something very badly, you will go to a lot of trouble to make it happen.

Ezra's dream was to know the law of the Lord. (The law of the Lord is the Word of God.) He decided that he would study the law of the Lord. You and I must also learn the Lord's Word with devotion.

He also wanted to learn the Word of God so that he could live it. Follow Ezra's example.

THE LORD ALWAYS WINS

They hired counselors to work against them and frustrate their plans. (Ezra 4:5)

When Ezra came from Persia to rebuild the temple, the devil tried to put a stop to it. He knew that if the temple was rebuilt, the Israelites would praise and serve the Lord.

The people who were not satisfied with the building of the temple first told Ezra that they would help build. But Ezra knew that they were actually enemies, and he did not want to allow them to help with the work. Then the enemies tried to frighten the builders and discourage them from going on with the building operations.

Fortunately, the Lord saw to it that the devil's plan to stop building altogether did not work.

If you serve the Lord you will notice that people will try to discourage and frighten you. Don't worry. The Lord always wins.

BE STRONG, BE BRAVE

Be strong and courageous. Do not be afraid ... for there is a greater power with us than with him. (2 Chronicles 32:7)

Hezekiah was a king of Israel. He reigned in Jerusalem almost thirty years. He was a good king and really wanted to serve the Lord. One of the wonderful things he did was to clean up the house of the Lord.

Then a king of another foreign country came on the scene. He invaded Israel and he wanted to put an end to Hezekiah's rule. Hezekiah had faith in God, and so he spoke to his army, "Be strong and courageous. Do not be afraid or discouraged because of the king of Assyria and the vast army with him, for there is a greater power with us than with him. With him is only the arm of flesh, but with us is the LORD our God to help us and to fight our battles" (verses 7-8).

If you are on God's side, you will ultimately win. Put your trust in Him today.

PASSING THE TEST

*God left him to test him and to know every-
thing that was in his heart.*
(2 Chronicles 32:31)

King Hezekiah was a rich and respected man. He became seriously ill, and he prayed to God. God miraculously healed him. But Hezekiah was not thankful that God had mercy on him. He started feeling self-satisfied. He started boasting.

One day God decided to test Hezekiah and left him. When God leaves you and me, things get very bad for us. God did this so that Hezekiah could know his own heart – his attitude and his feelings toward God. This is what the Lord tests. And Hezekiah's heart was not altogether what it should be.

Test your heart today. Is your attitude toward the Lord what it should be? Is there pride in your heart? Or sin? Confess it!

LAW AND ORDER

Thanksgiving must be made for everyone ... for kings and those in authority.
(1 Timothy 2:1, 2)

In every country there are people who maintain or keep order. It is usually done by the police and traffic officers. All people who have to maintain order are important. It is God's will that there must be order in a country, or in a town, or in a school. That is why we have to obey police officers and pray for them.

When two people have a disagreement, a judge must decide who is in the wrong and who is right. This is decided in a court of law. This is where people are tried. We must pray for those whose job is to pass judgment. We must pray that they will be fair and decide according to God's will.

Thank the Lord now for those who help with law and order and justice in our country.

WE WANT TO BE LIKE THEM

"Then we will be like all the other nations."
(1 Samuel 8:20)

We often see things others have and then wish we could have the same. The Israelites saw that the other nations had a king and they wanted one too.

Having a human king was unnecessary because they had the best King, God Himself. He had led them out of Egypt and He had given them the Ten Commandments. He ruled over them and He wanted to keep it that way, but they did not want to. Samuel warned them that it would not be the best thing for them to have a man for a king. Later on because of the disobedience of the kings, the people of Israel often suffered.

Don't want something just because someone else has it. Ask the Lord what His will is, and trust that He knows best.

THE ARK OF THE COVENANT

"Have them make a chest of acacia wood."
(Exodus 25:10)

God told the Israelites to make a box called the Ark of the Covenant. It was covered with pure gold and made of acacia wood. It was a sign that God was with them.

The Ark was usually placed in a tent, the tabernacle, and there the people worshiped God. When the people moved on, they picked up the Ark and carried it along with them. In this way they knew God went with them.

You and I don't need an Ark anymore to carry around with us. Neither do we need to pitch a tent or go to a particular building to meet God. We serve Him right inside of us if we open the doors of our lives for Him. He goes wherever we go. Serve the Lord today with your life.

IS HE GOING WITH YOU?

But if the cloud did not lift, they did not set out – until the day it lifted. (Exodus 40:37)

Whenever the Israelites reached a place where they were to spend the night, they pitched camp. They also put up the tabernacle, and put the Ark inside. Then something wonderful would happen: a cloud would cover the tabernacle, and the mighty presence of the Lord would fill the tent. The cloud stayed there until God wanted them to go on. When the cloud lifted from the tabernacle, the people knew they had to move on. If the cloud did not lift, they stayed there until it did. If they were to move without the cloud, God would not be with them. Then they would be in trouble.

Learn today that you shouldn't just do things without first making sure God will go with you.

OFFERINGS TO GOD

"When any of you brings an offering to the LORD ... " (Leviticus 1:2)

The Israelites had many offerings that they made to God. There were grain offerings, peace offerings and others. An offering was brought because the Israelites were sinful, and needed to answer to God for their sins. Offerings were also brought to God because it was a way of thanking Him.

The Old Testament offering is not in use any more. Does this mean that we no longer have to give the Lord anything? Does it mean that we no longer have sins that need to be taken away?

Jesus brought an offering in our place. His offering pays for our sins. We need just accept it. The thanks offering that you and I can bring now is the offering of our hearts and our lives.

"CHRISTIANS"

The disciples were called Christians first at Antioch. (Acts 11:26)

Christians are people who follow Christ, and because we are His followers, we also take His name. It was in Antioch that people were called Christians for the first time, because they told and showed everybody that they belonged to Christ.

Actually it is wrong to call someone a Christian if that person does not know and follow Christ. Many people are only Christians in name. If we want to call ourselves Christians, we must follow Christ.

If Christ means "the anointed one," then Christians are also "anointed ones." That is why the Holy Spirit anointed us. Like the fragrant anointing oil of the olden days, you and I must spread the fragrance of the gospel to everybody around us. Live like a true Christian today.

GOD'S THOUGHTS

*"As the heavens are higher than the earth,
so are My ways higher than your ways and
My thoughts than your thoughts."*
(Isaiah 55:8)

We often think wrong thoughts. Sometimes we think we are right, but we are actually wrong. Because we don't know everything, we often think just as far as we know. Because we don't have more facts, our thoughts are limited. God is not limited. He knows everything and He sees everything and what He thinks is perfect.

His thoughts are not like our thoughts. He looks differently at what we want. He sees the whole picture. He knows if what we ask Him for will be good for us to have or not. And if He decides we are not to have it, it is because He knows best.

CHICKEN OR EAGLE?

They will soar on wings like eagles.
(Isaiah 40:31)

C hickens are very different from eagles. Chickens can't really fly. By the time a chicken gets airborne, he's on his way down again!

An eagle is a majestic bird. He can fly magnificently and ride the wind for hours on end. An eagle is very strong and fast.

God wants us to be like eagles. That is why He says that if we put our trust in Him we will be given new strength, and we will take off like eagles. He wants us to reach new heights because He gives us the strength to do so. He does not want us to move awkwardly, like chickens. God's strength helps us to be winners.

Listen to the voice of the Lord today, allow His Spirit to fill you and soar with the eagle wings of faith.

FOOLISH PEOPLE

These people are ever hearing, but never understanding. (Isaiah 6:9)

The Lord said His people, Israel, were foolish. He taught them certain things, and although they heard what He said and seemed to understand, they didn't do what He said. This is being foolish: when you hear things and even understand, but still you don't want to do whatever you are told to do, especially if it will be good for you. It is almost like someone who doesn't eat and goes hungry even though there is plenty of food. Israel was like this. They were "never understanding." They did not want to do the right things.

You and I must ask the Lord to help us so that we will not be foolish when it comes to His things. Ask Him to make you diligent and willing and also smart, so that you can know His will and do it.

A PLACE WITH NO FEAR

The wolf and the lamb will live together. The baby will play safely near the hole of a cobra. (Isaiah 11:6, 8, NLT)

We live in a world where there are dangerous animals who hunt and kill. Lions prey on antelopes and snakes kill prey with their venom. We are scared of wild animals and with good reason.

Isaiah prophesies that a time will come when people will not fear snakes anymore. Babies will be allowed to play near the nest of a cobra. Antelope will no longer be afraid of leopards; they will live together. He is talking about heaven. We can look forward to living together with everything we were afraid of, because there will not be any fear or danger in heaven.

Thank the Lord that He makes it possible for us to look forward to a place where there will be no more evil or fear.

TO LOVE AND OBEY

Love the LORD your God and keep His requirements. (Deuteronomy 11:1)

When we love someone, we want to do what makes that person happy. If you love your mom and you know she expects you to behave in a certain manner, you show your love for her by being obedient and doing what she wants you to.

If we love God, we will do what He asks us to. The best reason for loving God is because He sent us His Son Jesus, and Jesus was prepared to give His whole life for us. He was tortured and hurt, but He died on the cross for you and me. God loves us so much that He gave us His Son. Because He loved us first, we love Him back.

Show your love by doing what He wants you to.

GIVING EVERYTHING

"This poor widow has put more into the treasury than all the others." (Mark 12:43)

One day Jesus saw people putting their money into the temple treasury. Rich people came past and gave a lot of money. Then Jesus saw a poor widow. She gave two small coins. Calling His disciples closer, Jesus said that the widow had given the most.

Jesus knew the rich people had so much money that they would hardly miss what they gave. The poor widow, on the other hand, was so poor that she couldn't even really afford to give anything; she needed the money for food. But because she loved God, she gave everything she had.

God likes us to give because we love. Give God everything today. Remember also, whenever you get a little money, give a little something for God's work.

JUDAS' WEAKNESS

With the reward he got for his wickedness,
Judas bought a field. (Acts 1:18)

Jesus chose Judas to follow Him. Judas took care of the money matters of the disciples. But Judas had a weakness.

Every one of us has a weak spot. Some people get angry very quickly. Others are greedy, and they will do something wrong to get hold of what they want. Some people are too proud. They think they are better than others. Judas liked money; he was greedy. He always wanted more and more.

The Pharisees bribed Judas with money to hand Jesus over to them. Later on Judas felt very bad about this. He bought himself a piece of property and hanged himself.

Ask the Lord what your weakness is. Ask Him to make you strong so that your weakness will not tempt you to do the wrong thing.

STOP DOUBTING

"Stop doubting and believe." (John 20:27)

After His death and resurrection, Jesus appeared to His disciples. Thomas was not with the other disciples at the time. The first thing the disciples told him when they saw him again was that they had seen Jesus.

Thomas did not believe that Jesus had risen from the dead. He said that if he didn't see the nail marks in Jesus' hands, he would never believe it. Eight days later Jesus appeared to His disciples again, and this time Thomas was with them. Jesus said to Thomas, "Put your finger here; see My hands ... Stop doubting and believe" (verse 27). Right then Thomas went down on his knees and worshiped Jesus.

You and I must not doubt like Thomas. Jesus said He would rise from the grave, but Thomas did not believe it. We can believe everything that Jesus says in His Word.

ALL THAT IMPORTANT?

"How hard it is for the rich to enter the kingdom of God." (Luke 18:24)

There was a rich young man whose money and possessions were more important to him than anything else. Yet, deep inside his heart he had a need. He came to Jesus and asked Him how he could get everlasting life. Jesus told him to sell all his belongings and follow Him. This was difficult for the young man to accept, because he was not prepared to do what Jesus said. Money was too important to him.

Money is important because we need things to stay alive. But money is not as important as knowing the Lord, following Him, and being rich inside. We are rich if we do God's will and experience what He gives so plentifully. Make sure that money doesn't become the most important thing in your life.

DON'T STRESS

"Who of you by worrying can add a single hour to his life?" (Matthew 6:27)

Some people worry about anything and everything. They lie awake nights about the things they fear.

We all have our worries at times. Yes, we do worry about things that can go wrong. Yet the Bible tells us that we should not get into the bad habit of worrying about everything. Jesus said to His disciples, "do not worry about your life" (verse 25). He also questioned them, asking if it was possible that a person's worries could make him live even one hour longer. As a matter of fact, all the knowledgeable people tell us that worry makes us stressed, and that makes us unhappy. Stress can also make our bodies ill.

Learn to put your trust in the Lord and thank Him for everything. Don't get stressed out!

THEY FORGOT

*But they did not understand what He was
saying to them. (Luke 2:50)*

Mary and Joseph knew that Jesus was
the Son of God. When Jesus was
twelve years old, He went with His family
to Jerusalem for Passover. On the way back
home Mary and Joseph started to look
for Jesus and could not find Him. Three
days later they found Him at the temple
in Jerusalem where He was talking to the
learned people. His parents asked Him why
He had left them. Jesus answered, "Didn't
you know I had to be in My Father's house?"
(verse 49).

Mary and Joseph did not quite understand what He meant. For a moment they
forgot that He was the Son of God and not
like other children.

Even if there are things you don't understand, just trust God. He knows best.

ARE YOU ASHAMED?

I am not ashamed of the gospel, because it is the power of God for the salvation of everyone who believes. (Romans 1:16)

Christians identify with Christ. We have accepted Him as Savior and Lord. When you are still a young Christian, you might sometimes be embarrassed to tell others that you belong to Jesus.

As you get stronger and grow in Jesus, it becomes easier to admit openly that you are His follower. You know, as Paul did, that it is nothing to be ashamed of. We should rather be very happy and talk about it, because then it can also help others confess their sins. Jesus' message is a happy message. Share it with others without being ashamed so that they can find out for themselves how wonderful it is to know Him.

THEY LAUGHED

But they laughed at Him. (Mark 5:40)

One day Jesus was busy healing people, when the synagogue leader was told that his little girl had died. Jesus heard this sad message and He told the leader, "Don't be afraid; just believe" (verse 36). Jesus went to the house of the leader and saw the people there weeping bitterly. Jesus told them the little girl had not died but was just sleeping. They laughed at Him, mocked Him, and scorned Him. They had seen for themselves the child was dead. Then Jesus took the child by the hand. When He told her to get up, she did just that. Everybody was speechless with surprise.

Today there are still many people who scorn the message of Jesus. They laugh and say the Bible is just stories. But we know the truth. Pray that people will not laugh at God, but will praise Him.

USING WHAT YOU HAVE

"Well done You have been faithful with a few things; I will put you in charge of many things." (Matthew 25:21)

Jesus told the story of a man who was going on a journey and asked three of his workers to look after his property. He gave one worker five gold coins, another one two, and the third received one coin. The master told them to use what he had entrusted to them in the best way.

When the master came back from his journey, he praised the first two workers, but he was fed up with the last worker who had not put his money to good use. With this story, Jesus wants to give us a message: We must develop the talents He has given us and use them well for His glory.

Thank the Lord for everything He has given you. Don't bury your talents.

NO FAVORITES

"You are impartial and don't play favorites." (Matthew 22:16, NLT)

We treat people as if some are more important than others. I know there are people who are important because of their rank or position, but God has no favorites. All people are equal before God.

The Pharisees saw that Jesus did not favor certain people and ignore others. "We know you are a man of integrity and that you teach ... in accordance with the truth. You aren't swayed by men, because you pay no attention to who they are" (verse 16).

Remember that you are just as important to the Lord as any other person. If Jesus likes you it is not because you are pretty or good. He loves you and cares for you. You don't need to impress Him. Just be yourself. Decide to serve Him with all your heart.

KING ON A DONKEY

"See, your king comes to you, gentle and riding on a donkey, on a colt, the foal of a donkey." (Matthew 21:5)

Donkeys are humble animals. People used to put their goods on a donkey's back and then walked alongside the donkey from one place to another.

Jesus decided to ride into Jerusalem on a donkey. Jesus is the King of kings and yet He rode into Jerusalem on the back of a donkey. The king of our lives, Jesus Christ, is not haughty or boastful. He is humble. Doesn't the fact that He came down from heaven to live on earth prove that He is humble? He, the Son of God, was prepared to become human, a human like us.

As the children of a humble king like Jesus, we must also behave humbly. We must not think too much of ourselves.

A GREAT HERITAGE

Surely I have a delightful inheritance.
(Psalm 16:6)

Sometimes we should think about things and people that have come before us. Our heritage is things that we have inherited and that have been passed down to us.

There are people in this country whose families have lived here for centuries. Your grandfather and grandmother and their grandfathers and grandmothers before them most probably lived here, and they passed certain things down to you, like your language, your religion, and all kinds of everyday things.

You and I can thank the Lord for all the good things we have received. Everything comes from the hand of the Lord, but there are also people who worked hard to keep what the Lord gave them in a good condition for you and me.

GOD WILLING

Do not boast about tomorrow.
(Proverbs 27:1)

It is good to have plans for the future, but we must not be so excited about tomorrow that we don't live today.

The Bible says you must not boast about what you expect tomorrow. Whoever boasts about tomorrow pretends that he or she has already received what must still come tomorrow. That is dangerous. How can we know what is waiting for us tomorrow? We don't even know what is going to happen to us in the next hour. That is why Christians say, "God willing ... " This saying means that it all depends on the Lord if we will have a tomorrow. Perhaps you have heard someone say, "DV." This is short for the Latin *Deo Volente*, which means "if God is willing."

Are you looking forward to something? Then remind yourself, if God is willing.

GOOD FOR EVIL

If your enemy is hungry, give him food to eat. (Proverbs 25:21)

If someone doesn't like us, it is very easy not to like that person. If someone is cross with us, it is just as easy to be cross with that person. God's way is different. He says we must love our enemies; we must not hate them. If someone who hates us is hungry, we must give him something to eat.

Only God can help us to love people like this. It is also a very good way to show that we love Jesus and belong to Him. We must not return evil for evil. Ask the Lord to help you show love to that person. Perhaps the love you show him or her will make that person stop hating you, and it will please God if the heart of such a person is changed.

FILLED WITH PEACE

A heart at peace gives life to the body.
(Proverbs 14:30)

Our heart is the place deep down where we feel. Sometimes we feel good, sometimes not so good. Sometimes we feel excited, and sometimes we are calm and relaxed. When we are scared, our hearts are filled with fear. If we are glad, our hearts are full of joy. If we are anxious, our hearts are stormy, almost like the waves of the sea that can't stop breaking.

It is not good for us if we are anxious all the time. Restlessness, worry, and fear are all things that upset us, and they are not good for our bodies. It is much better to be calm and restful.

The Lord helps you to have peace in your heart. Give Him all your worries, pray to Him, and trust Him. He will fill you with His peace. This will also help make your body healthier.

IN THE BREACH

Moses ... stood in the breach before him.
(Psalm 106:23)

We read in Psalm 106 how the people of Israel forgot God, their Savior. They were wicked and rebellious. The Lord was very angry with them and decided to destroy them.

Moses was prepared to speak to God on behalf of these people. He "stood in the breach" for Israel which means that he asked God to forgive them. Just because one man prayed, the lives of thousands and thousands of people were spared.

We can also stand in the breach for others. There are many people who live under God's judgment because they reject Jesus, but you and I can pray for them, plead for them, and ask the Lord to change their hearts and spare their lives.

If you see someone disobeying God, stand in the breach for them.

CONTENT AND SATISFIED

If we have food and clothing, we will be content with that. (1 Timothy 6:8)

To be satisfied with what you have is a wonderful characteristic. Some people have so much, and yet they are never satisfied. Others have very little, yet they are content and satisfied.

The Bible says if we have food and clothes we have nothing to complain about. Food keeps us alive, and clothes keep us warm and protected. It is as if the Bible is saying that if we have the basic things in life, we can be happy. We are satisfied because we are thankful for what we have received. The Lord promised that He would give us food and clothing if we put our trust in Him. Children of the Lord should never be dissatisfied.

Take time now to thank the Lord for everything you have.

THE NURSE

"Let us look for a young [girl] to attend the king and take care of him." (1 Kings 1:2)

When King David was old, he suffered a lot. His servants chose a nurse who could be with him every minute of the day and night to take care of him. From all the girls, they chose Abishag. She was very young and also very pretty. She saw to all his needs and looked after him well.

Today nurses still care for sick people. It is a wonderful job because nurses care for those in need. They make sure that the sick are well taken care of. They also help the doctors who treat their patients.

Thank the Lord for nurses. Many of them are also Christians, and they care not only for the bodies of the sick, but also talk to them, encourage them, and tell them about Jesus. Pray for nurses today.

ROAD SIGNS

"Set up road signs; put up guideposts."
(Jeremiah 31:21)

Road signs tell us which way to go and if there is any danger ahead. They are there to help us as we travel.

God told His people to set up road signs and guideposts to make sure they reach the right destination. You and I also need road signs and signposts that show us the way. What road signs are these?

Examples of road signs for you and me are pastors, youth leaders and teachers. They could also be good advice from friends, counseling from our parents, and, of course, the Word of God and the Holy Spirit. Take note of all these road signs and obey them. Put up your sign posts, keep your eyes on the main road, and don't wander off in your own direction.

WHO DOES HE THINK HE IS?

And they took offense at Him. (Mark 6:3)

Jesus did many wonderful miracles and taught amazing and wise lessons, but in His own home town they didn't want anything to do with Him. They asked one another, "Isn't this the carpenter? Isn't this Mary's son and the brother of James ... Aren't his sisters here with us?" (verse 3).

It was because they had known Jesus since childhood that they didn't take Him seriously. They thought of Him as an ordinary person because He grew up before their eyes.

Perhaps you are finding it difficult to follow Jesus in your own home, but just keep at it, even if your own family is negative and discourages you. The same thing happened to Jesus. You just go on praying for your family and friends.

CHEERED UP

For they refreshed my spirit …
(1 Corinthians 16:18)

Paul did wonderful work for God and worked very hard. Sometimes he worked so hard that he became very tired in both body and soul.

Paul was very glad when three friends came to visit him. They refreshed his spirit; in other words, they cheered him up. After this visit, Paul was filled with new courage and strength for all the work he had to do for the Lord.

You and I also need friends who can be with us when we need encouragement and cheering up. Good friends are like a cool glass of water when you are thirsty. They refresh you and make you feel much better. Thank the Lord for your friends who are there for you and cheer you up when you need it. Be a friend like this to others.

THE THORN

There was given me a thorn in my flesh.
(2 Corinthians 12:7)

Have you ever had a thorn in your foot? It hurts! Paul spoke about a thorn in his flesh. This was not a real thorn, but some hurt or difficulty in his life. We don't really know what it was. It could have been an illness, deformity or weak eyes. Three times he asked the Lord to take this away. The Lord's answer was short and sweet: "My grace is sufficient for you" (verse 9). Later on Paul writes that he knows he has this problem to keep him humble. It made him realize that he needed God.

Is there something that makes your life difficult? Perhaps you also want the Lord to take it away. Perhaps this difficulty is there for the same reason as Paul's. One thing we know: the Lord's grace is enough for us. Yes, He carries us through and supports us.

WHERE IS DEMAS?

Demas, because he loved this world, has deserted me. (2 Timothy 4:10)

Demas was a Christian, and at first he served the Lord with all his heart. Then something went wrong, because Paul writes that Demas decided to leave him. Paul says the reason was that Demas loved the world.

When the Bible talks about "the world," it means everything that is not the will of God. There are many good and wonderful things in life, and also many wonderful people. But if they do not accept Jesus as King and Lord, they are part of "the world." Often it is all the glitz and glamour of a world without Christ that seems so inviting to us. To Demas it was so attractive that he decided not to serve the Lord anymore. He loved things better than the Lord and His kingdom. What a shame!

JUST YOU

No one came to my support, but everyone deserted me. (2 Timothy 4:16)

Has anybody ever let you down? Have you ever ended up alone with a problem because everybody disappeared when the work had to be done? It happened to Paul in the Bible.

Paul served the Lord with his whole being. Many of his friends left him. Perhaps they were afraid, or some may have been embarrassed. Paul says when he had to appear in court the first time no one was there to support him. Can you think how unhappy that must have made him? He even ended up in prison.

Yet, just listen what Paul adds: "But the Lord stood at my side and gave me strength … I was delivered from the lion's mouth" (verse 17). Even if people let you down and disappoint you, the Lord stays at your side. He will support you.

DO YOU LOVE?

"A new command I give you: Love one another." (John 13:34)

The Bible sees true love as a command from the Lord. Because the Lord tells us to love one another, we must love one another; it's as simple as that. Love is not a feeling. It is a choice. This means that you and I must say, "We will love because God tells us to."

Love is one of God's commandments, and it means that I must do deeds of love for all people, whether I like them or not. The question is not how we feel about people; the question is whether we are prepared to love them as Jesus loves them.

Even if we don't like them, we should help them, support them, and want what's best for them. Decide that you will love all people that you meet today, even if you don't like them.

RESPECT YOUR PARENTS

"Honor your father and your mother."
(Exodus 20:12)

God has given us parents to look after us and to take care of our needs. Our parents are there for us right from the start and want what is best for us. This means that they make life fun and entertaining, but it also means that they discipline us. They want us to grow up to be good citizens and people who do what is right.

Christian parents want us to know God and serve Him with our whole hearts so they teach us what the Bible says and what Jesus would do.

When your parents discipline you, try to not get angry with them. They are only trying to teach you the right ways. They only punish you because they love you and want you to be the best you can be. Thank God for your parents.

ABRAHAM'S BIG TEST

The LORD Will Provide (Genesis 22:14)

When Isaac was a young boy, the Lord told Abraham to sacrifice his son. God wanted to test Abraham's love for Him.

Abraham did what God had told him to do. He saddled his donkey and chopped wood for the burnt offering. Isaac asked his father what animal they were going to sacrifice. Abraham answered that the Lord would provide. When they reached the place of sacrifice, he tied up his son and placed him on the altar.

Just as Abraham took the knife to slaughter his son, an angel of the Lord called down from heaven and told him to stop. Then the Lord said, "Now I know that you fear God, because you have not withheld from me your son, your only son" (verse 12).

How much do you love God?

THE GRACE OF JESUS

May the grace of the Lord Jesus Christ ... be with you all. (2 Corinthians 13:14)

Paul often ended his letters with words similar to those above. The word *grace* comes from the Greek word *charis*, and in its simplest form it means simply "gifts." Paul is praying that all the gifts that Jesus wants to hand out to us with His death and resurrection will become real in our lives. Which gifts?

Jesus saw to it that you and I are saved through His life and death and everything He came to do for us, that we are forgiven and made new, and that we receive the fruit of the Holy Spirit and much more. All these are spiritual gifts or "mercy" that the Lord gives us.

My prayer is that you will receive the grace-gift of Jesus in your life.

THE GIFT OF LOVE

May ... the love of God ... be with you all.
(2 Corinthians 13:14)

Yesterday we saw that Paul's blessing was something he wished for his Christian friends. He did not pray that they would receive Jesus' grace-gift only, but also the love of God.

Without God's love you and I cannot live meaningful lives. We need God's love. His love makes us strong. His love changes our lives. God proved His love for us when He gave us His Son. He loved us too much to allow us to perish, and that is why He sent Jesus. Yes, He proves His love through Jesus on the cross. It is this love that He also wants to give to you and me today.

He wants you to know now that He loves you very much, that He cares about you, and that He will be with you in everything you do.

WHAT IS FELLOWSHIP?

May ... the fellowship of the Holy Spirit be with you all. (2 Corinthians 13:14)

The last part of the blessing with which Paul ended his letters mentions fellowship. He prays that people will experience the fellowship of the Holy Spirit. What does this mean?

When someone is a child of God and has accepted Jesus Christ as Savior, that person has the Holy Spirit. All Christians have this in common: they have the Holy Spirit in their hearts and lives. This unites them, leads them in truth, fulfills them, and gives them the fruit and gifts they need. The Holy Spirit is like an invisible person in our hearts, and this makes it so that we look at things in the same way.

This is how Christians can live together in harmony: They have the same Spirit who encourages them to love one another.

JESUS AND THE WHIP

Jesus made a whip from some ropes and chased them all out of the Temple.
(John 2:15, NLT)

Jesus was angry because the temple, where people were supposed to worship, was beginning to look like a supermarket. The main reason people were coming to the temple was not to pray anymore, but to make a lot of money. Jesus was angry and disappointed. He made a whip and chased out of the temple all those people who were buying and selling, along with their sheep and cattle. The news probably spread that Jesus was whipping people. Jesus did not care what the people thought of Him. He wanted what was right.

We must also take a firm stand on things that are not right. It doesn't mean we have to whip people, but we need to be very firm out of respect for God.

WHAT'S DONE IS DONE

But one thing I do: Forgetting what is behind and straining toward what is ahead.
(Philippians 3:13)

We all have things that happened in our past that we don't like thinking about. The good news is that it's over.

Paul was very sorry about his past. He had people killed because he thought it was wrong to follow Jesus. That was a big mistake, but he could not make it go away. He was a murderer. Then God changed his heart, and Paul became a Christian. He asked God to forgive him, and he decided, "I am forgetting what is behind and looking toward what is ahead."

Do the same. Don't keep thinking about past failures and sins. Free yourself from things that happened yesterday. If you have confessed your sins, you are forgiven. Look forward to the future.

BEFORE YOU WERE BORN

Your eyes saw my unformed body.
(Psalm 139:16)

It is wonderful to know that the Lord had a plan for your life long before you were born. Even before your birth the Lord had already decided what your name would be, what you would look like, which talents He would give you, and what His plan for your life would be. King David realized that he was not simply one man among many, but that the Lord knew him personally, long before his birth.

Who you are and what you look like are all part of God's plan for your life. Thank Him for all your talents and for what you are, even if you are not all that happy with yourself. Praise and thank the Lord that He knew all about you even before you were born. Decide today to live for Him and His kingdom.

A SPECIAL WEDDING

For the wedding of the Lamb has come, and
His bride has made herself ready.
(Revelation 19:7)

A wedding is an exciting and festive occasion. The bride spends a lot of time doing her hair and makeup and then putting on a stunning wedding dress. The groom looks sharp, because this wedding day is a very important day.

In Revelation 19 we read about a very special wedding. It is called the "wedding of the Lamb." The Lamb is Jesus Christ. The Bible says Jesus is like a groom. And who is the bride? You and me! Every one of us who belongs to Jesus is Jesus' bride. One day He will come and get us and we will be "married" to Him in heaven. Yes, we will be with Him forever and ever. There we will celebrate and be joyful. Are you ready for the heavenly wedding?

THE OPEN DOOR

*See, I have placed before you an open door
that no one can shut. (Revelation 3:8)*

When you turn the key in a strong deadbolt, the door is locked so securely that it is very difficult to open it without the key.

In this verse God is telling us that He alone can open or shut a door for us. Often we want to open a "door" ourselves. Say, you want to play the lead in the school play and you try just about everything to get that role. Or you so badly want to play in the team for your school that you try everything to make that team. You try opening the "door" to that team.

Rather, you should ask God to open and shut doors for you. If He opens a door for you, no one on earth will ever close it again.

READY FOR HARVESTING

"The harvest is plentiful, but the workers are few." (Luke 10:2)

Farmers work very hard to prepare their land before they sow seeds. All the preparation must be done before the plants can produce a crop. Jesus also talks about a harvest field. A cornfield is green at first while the corn grows, and later the grain growing on the ears becomes yellow. Then it is ready for harvesting.

The billions of people on earth are like uncountable ears of corn. God says, "See, they are ripe in the fields." We must tell them they can be saved and go to heaven – that they can be given a new life.

We must not only pray for the billions of people who have not even heard about Jesus; we must be prepared to tell them about Jesus. We must be like workers, willing to harvest.

GOD'S WORKERS

" ... to send out workers into His harvest field." (Matthew 9:38)

Every worker on a farm has his or her own specific task. Some drive tractors. Others must bag up the grain. Others fasten the bags, or load and unload the bags.

You and I are workers in the Lord's service, and we also have a task. Some are pastors, others have a specific duty to perform in the church, and some are singers. Others take part in prayer meetings or talk to people about Jesus. Then there are those whose calling is to be witnesses for the Lord as doctors, nurses, or businesspeople. We all have a task to carry out. In this way God's bumper crop is harvested because each of us is a worker in God's huge field.

We must also pull our weight. We are workers, and we have to help harvest the Lord's crop.

A CUP OF COLD WATER

"If you give even a cup of cold water to one of the least of My followers, you will surely be rewarded." (Matthew 10:42)

We must help people who work full-time for the Lord and try to make their task easier. We must give them our support, give them money when necessary, and see that they get what they need to do the Lord's work. Even if we give them a cup of cold water when they are thirsty, the Lord sees it, and He will reward us.

Think of ways to help those who work for the Lord. Perhaps you can pray for them. Perhaps you can give them a hand and encourage them. You can invite them to join you for a meal at your house. If we support people in this way, it is as if we are doing it for Jesus Himself.

NEVER WORTHLESS

"A bruised reed He will not break, and a smoldering wick He will not snuff out."
(Matthew 12:20)

In Bible times when people had to go through a river, they used a reed to show them how deep the water was. But a bent reed was no good to use.

They also used lamps that were filled with oil. Inside the lamp was a wick, and it was the wick that burned and made the light. Sometimes the wick started smoldering and smoking. Then it was better to put it out, otherwise the whole house would be full of unpleasant smoke.

Even if you and I sometimes feel as worthless as a bent reed and a smoldering wick, God will still be able to use us. Thank the Lord that He uses you in spite of all your shortcomings.

DON'T PULL THEM UP

"The servants asked him, 'Do you want us to go and pull them up?'" (Matthew 13:28)

Jesus told the story of a man who sowed good seed. One night when everyone was asleep, his enemy came and sowed weeds among the wheat. The farmer's servants asked him if they should pull up the weeds. He answered, "No ... because while you are pulling the weeds, you may root up the wheat with them. Let both grow together until the harvest. At that time I will tell the harvesters: First collect the weeds and tie them in bundles to be burned; then gather the wheat and bring it into my barn" (verse 29, 30). What did Jesus mean?

God knows everyone's heart. He knows who the weeds are – and who is wheat. Who truly believes in Him and who doesn't. We can trust Him to judge the weeds at the right time.

NO MORE QUESTIONS

"In that day you will no longer ask Me anything." (John 16:23)

Because we wonder about so many things, we ask a lot of questions. There are also many spiritual things we do not understand. Sometimes we ask our pastor to explain something that we don't understand. Some questions have clear and definite answers. Other questions are more difficult to answer. Only God knows all the answers.

Jesus says a day will come when you and I will not need to ask any more questions. In that day we will know all the answers. Everything that we couldn't understand before will be crystal clear to us. This is the day that we will be in heaven with God. We will know everything and understand everything. Until then we must believe and trust the Lord.

I HAVE TO PREACH

I am compelled to preach. Woe to me if I do not preach the gospel! (1 Corinthians 9:16)

The word gospel means "good news." Paul said he couldn't help preaching the good news of Jesus Christ. Everywhere he went he would tell people about Jesus and how to be saved.

Paul had a deep desire in his heart to preach the gospel. Do you remember that the Lord called him to do it? God gave him the specific task to preach the gospel to the gentile nations in particular. The Holy Spirit encouraged him.

Every one of God's children should, like Paul, have a longing to preach the gospel. Jesus wants the whole world to know about Him. We must preach the gospel. Woe to us if we do not do it! Ask God today to help you tell others about Him.

WILD PEOPLE

When people do not accept divine guidance, they run wild. (Proverbs 29:18, NLT)

Today's Scripture means that when the will of God is not made known to people they are uncontrolled and run wild. Wild horses are dangerous. If you try to ride one, it is very likely that it will throw you because it will buck and go wild.

Wild people are just as bad. When people run wild (often because they have had too much to drink), they do all kinds of very stupid things.

The Bible tells us that if the will of the Lord and the Word of God are not brought to the people, they become wild (they have no restraint). It is the Word of God that changes our hearts and our will, so that we become better people.

Pray that God's Word and His will may be preached in our country.

DON'T YOU KNOW ME?

"Don't you know me, Philip, even after I have been among you such a long time?"
(John 14:9)

Philip lived with Jesus and shared everything with Him. Philip heard Him talk about His kingdom. And then Philip made a strange request, "Lord, show us the Father ... "

This was when Jesus said that it seemed as if Philip didn't know Him even though he had been with Him such a long time.

The Lord speaks to us in many ways and in many places. Often we hear, but we don't really hear. I don't think the Lord minds that we ask Him questions, but I do think that He sometimes expects us to know more answers, seeing that we have His Word and we are His children.

Make an effort to get to know the Lord even better.

GO THE EXTRA MILE

"If someone forces you to go one mile, go with him two miles." (Matthew 5:41)

It is precisely when we must do things that we don't enjoy that we reveal Jesus' love and attitude. It is when we love our enemies that we glow with a wonderful testimony for all to see. It is when we serve others that people will ask why we are so different. Then we can tell them it is Jesus who taught us to be like Him.

We must amaze others with our loving ways – especially those who least expect it. Our enemies will be so surprised at a deed of love from the heart of God. Come, let's walk that extra mile without being asked. Then we will please the Lord, and we will be a bright light in the dark world.

COME A LITTLE CLOSER

Come near to God and He will come near to you. (James 4:8)

God wants us to be close to Him. Jesus' other name is *Immanuel*, meaning "God with us." Because God saw that we were far away from Him, He decided to send us His Son. In this way He came near us. James tells us that we must draw nearer to God: Draw near to Him and He will draw near to you.

This is a promise from God's Word. The arms of the Lord are always ready to receive us. He wants us to be very near to Him. When He is near to us, our hearts are full of peace, love, and true happiness.

Decide that you want to draw even closer to the Lord today. He is waiting for you with outstretched arms if you want to come near to Him.

FOR THE SAKE OF THE GOSPEL

I have become all things to all men so that by all possible means I might save some.
(1 Corinthians 9:22)

Paul knew that if he wanted to preach the gospel, he had to reach out to sinful people. This doesn't mean that he was prepared to sin; rather, it means that Paul saw to it that he was on the same level with his hearers. He talked to the Jews in their language, and to the Greeks in theirs. With children, he talked on a child's level. With clever people he used suitable language.

Jesus was also prepared to mingle with bad people so that He could speak to them and share the gospel.

We must reach out to others and speak to them about their interests, and when we get the opportunity, we must tell them about Jesus.

AFRAID, BUT OBEDIENT

Samuel ... was afraid to tell Eli the vision.
(1 Samuel 3:15)

One night as Samuel was sleeping, the Lord called him. Samuel answered, "Speak Lord, for Your servant is listening." Then the Lord spoke to Samuel and gave him a message for Eli. Unfortunately, it was not good news.

It couldn't have been easy for Samuel to give Eli this message. But he had to be obedient. Often we find it very difficult to tell someone the truth. Even if the truth hurts, we must tell it. But we must do it in love and obedience to the Lord.

If Samuel had not obeyed the Lord, Eli would not have been prepared for what was going to happen. Then Samuel would not have had peace with God. When the Lord asks us to do something, we must do it.

YOU MUST MOVE

Abraham obeyed and went, even though
he did not know where he was going.
(Hebrews 11:8)

God had a plan for Abraham's life and called him to move from Ur. Abraham obeyed even though he didn't know where to go.

The Lord calls many people to follow Him. He calls you too. The Lord doesn't tell us exactly where we're headed. What He does tell us is that He will be with us. What He is asking is that we trust Him. That is faith. Abraham believed that the Lord knew what He was doing, and so he moved away from Ur. Because Abraham believed, the Lord did wonderful things through him.

Every day must be a step along the road with Jesus. We don't know what will happen this day, but let's trust Him to show us the way.

LOOK TO THE HEAVENS

Look up into the heavens. Who created all the stars? (Isaiah 40:26, NLT)

When you see the wonders of the galaxy, you cannot help but realize that a great and mighty Creator made it all. We see so much of God's greatness in nature. We see Him in the mountains, in the flowers, and even in modern technology. If we allow our minds to open our eyes, we will see God in everything around us.

At school you learn about wonderful things. You take in new knowledge. If you read books and encyclopedias, you will get to know about the most interesting things. If you are a child of the Lord, you cannot help but see the hand of God in everything. You must thank and praise the Lord for all the wonderful things. He is the Creator and Lord of your life.

ALL DAY LONG

Pray continually. (1 Thessalonians 5:17)

Paul says we are to pray continually. Continually means all the time, without stopping. We are to pray continually when we talk to God in our thoughts all the time. We share everything with Him: what we see, what we hear, and what we experience. As the day goes on, we can talk to the Lord all the time about everything that is happening to us.

We can talk about our feelings. We can talk about things we want to see or have. We can say thank you for things we enjoy. We can pray for someone else. We can speak to the Lord if we feel we are in danger. Yes, we can really speak to God about everything.

Let's make it a way of life to talk to the Lord continually.

JEALOUSY AND QUARRELING

*For since there is jealousy and quarreling
among you, are you not worldly?*
(1 Corinthians 3:3)

Paul writes a letter to the Corinthians. They had accepted Jesus and were following Him. Yet they sometimes still acted like non-Christians. Even as Christians we still sometimes do things that God does not want us to do.

Paul writes that the Corinthians were sometimes jealous and quarreled with others. He says that when we are jealous or fighting with others, we are not acting like Christians, but like worldly people. Worldly people don't have the Holy Spirit in their hearts. They don't live according to the Word of God. So, we would expect them to fight and be jealous. We do not expect this behavior from Christians. Try to live in peace with all people, and don't begrudge them the good things in their lives.

WAKE UP

"Wake up, O sleeper, rise from the dead, and Christ will shine on you." (Ephesians 5:14)

Sleep is good for you. It gives you new strength. But if you are spiritually asleep, then it's not a good thing. The Bible says you must be spiritually awake.

This means that we must be on fire for the Lord. We must be diligent, wide awake, and serving the Lord with energy and lots of enthusiasm.

Spiritual sleep is almost like spiritual death. A person who is asleep is not active. There is no sign of real life as there is when someone runs or plays or sings or talks. The Lord does not want us to be spiritually dead. He wants us to be alive and lively; others must see that we know the Lord, that we love Him and follow Him, because our behavior shows it.

EVEN MORE FRUITFUL

"Every branch that does bear fruit He prunes so that it will be even more fruitful." (John 15:2)

You and I are like trees. If you can't see fruit on a tree, then it is not a fruitful tree. Our heavenly Father wants to see fruit on the tree of our lives so that He can be glorified.

God is a great gardener, and He prunes us so that we can bear more fruit in our lives. A tree is pruned so that it can produce more fruit. Pruning involves cutting off the things that are not good for us and this may not be pleasant for us, but God does it so that we can bear more fruit. The Lord wants to prune all bad things out of our lives, like bad habits and sinful thoughts. Because of God's pruning, we can bear better fruit.

HE WILL RECEIVE ME

Though my father and mother forsake me,
the LORD will receive me. (Psalm 27:10)

We all sometimes miss our parents when they are not with us for whatever reason. We are sometimes lonely because we cannot have our parents with us all the time. But the Bible has comfort for us. The Lord promises to take us in His care and says that He will be with us always. After all, His name is also Father. He is not an earthly father, that is true, but He is the heavenly Father who, in Jesus, is with us all the time.

He wants to take us in His Father's arms, and He assures us that He will take care of us. Thank the Lord that He, like your father and mother, will take you into His care and will be with you always.

HE GIVES BACK

"I will repay you for the years the locusts have eaten." (Joel 2:25)

In the time of the prophet Joel, the Lord sent a swarm of locusts to eat the Israelites' crops. A very difficult time lay ahead of them. God wanted to teach them a lesson. Yet He promised that He would give them His blessings again.

Often things happen in our lives that we find very difficult to accept. The Lord helps His children in times of hardship. One day in heaven, we will be given the perfect reward, when everything will be perfect and there will be no more tears and hurt.

The Lord is the great God of heaven and earth, and He will help us when things go wrong. You just put your trust in the Lord. Leave your life in His hands and know that He will take care of you.

IT IS OK TO CRY

Record my lament; list my tears on Your scroll. (Psalm 56:8)

Everyone cries at some stage. You cry with joy when you are happy about something. Heartache can make you cry. Or you can cry because you have been hurt.

They say it is good to cry. It is never good to bottle up our feelings. It is better to cry about things and get them out of our system than to keep them inside and pretend that nothing is wrong. Tears help to lighten our load. We must never be ashamed to cry. Of course we must not cry about every little thing, but if we really hurt it is all right to cry.

The Bible says that God keeps a record of all His children's tears. One day He will wipe the tears from our eyes, and there will be no more tears (see Revelation 21:4).

LOVING AND CARING

Each of you should not look not only to your own interests, but also to the interests of others. (Philippians 2:4)

People need people, and we must care for others. We are in a family and we can't pretend we don't need each other. If we have brothers or sisters in the same family, we are responsible for them in a special way. It is as if the Lord gives one to the other so that they can care for each other.

We must encourage each other and be loving and caring, and we should also show each other in a nice way where we each go wrong.

Cain hated his brother Abel. This is not the way to behave. We must not walk around with mean thoughts toward our brothers and sisters. We must pray for them and love them.

CROUCHING AT THE DOOR

"Sin is crouching at the door, eager to control you. But you must subdue it and be its master." (Genesis 4:7, NLT)

As long as we are on earth sin will be a problem. It is as if sin is crouching out there, waiting to pounce.

God says that you must subdue sin. Although the possibility of sin is always there, so is the possibility of saying no. That is often the most difficult thing to do. We must ask the Lord to help us.

Often sin comes in the form of something so inviting that you find it very difficult to say no. Ask the Lord to help you and to give you the wisdom to recognize sin when it uses sly ways of getting to you. If we are willing, the Lord will help us to master sin.

ONE BAD APPLE

He who walks with the wise grows wise,
but a companion of fools suffers harm.
(Proverbs 13:20)

If there is one bad apple in a box, all the others go bad quicker, and before you know it there is not one good apple left.

There is a saying, "He who sleeps with dogs gets up with fleas." We are all influenced by one another, and that is why it is important who your friends are. You are the way your friends are. If your friends have bad habits, it will be easy for you to pick up these habits. It is almost like the apples in the box. If we keep company with wise people and listen to them, we also become wise.

We want to be wise and do what is right. Choose Christians for friends so that they can have a good influence on you.

HAPPY TO GO

I rejoiced with those who said to me, "Let us go to the house of the Lord." (Psalm 122:1)

David was very pleased when his friends said, "Let's go to the house of the Lord." David knew that in the house of the Lord God would talk to him.

Today the church is not the only house of the Lord. The Lord now lives in our hearts. God's house is in our bodies. Our bodies are the temple of the Holy Spirit. Wherever we go, God goes with us. Still, we go to church to listen to the Word of God together with other Christians; we encourage and uplift one another. There we pray and sing together to the glory of God.

If you love the Lord, you want to be where He is praised and where His Word is preached.

SHINING EVER BRIGHTER

The path of the righteous is like the first gleam of dawn, shining ever brighter till the full light of day. (Proverbs 4:18)

One of the wonderful things about being a Christian is that we are lit up by the light of Christ shining ever brighter as we go along.

When we accept Jesus, His light is in our heart. The further we walk the road of life with Him, the brighter His light in our hearts and life. At first our life is like the first gleam of dawn in the morning, before sunrise. Later on the sun rises and soon it is bright daylight. Such is the life of a person who lives with the Lord.

The longer we live with Him, the brighter His light shines in our life. Let the Lord's sunshine light up your life today.

WHAT ARE YOU WEARING?

Before me was a great multitude that no one could count ... They were wearing white robes. (Revelation 7:9)

You dress to suit where you are going and what you are doing. You might have to wear a uniform to school. When you play sports, you wear sports clothes. When you go to a wedding you wear your best outfit.

What must we wear for the Lord? Not ordinary clothes, like a suit or a pretty dress. No, the Bible talks about clean, white clothes. This is an image to say we must be washed clean of sin. In Revelation we read that people standing before the Lord were dressed in white clothes.

When the Lord washes you clean from sin, you will be given sparkling clean, white redemption clothes. When you are dressed properly you can enter into the presence of the Lord joyfully.

LOVE THE RIGHT WAY

For love is as strong as death.
(Song of Songs 8:6)

Song of Songs is a beautiful book in the Bible. It is a song written about the love between a man and a woman. In this book we read how much the man loves the woman of his dreams, and the woman tells how wonderful the man is that she loves.

Because love is such a strong feeling, the devil can make use of it as well. That is a pity. Often people fall in love, but then they become very jealous. People have even committed murder because of jealousy.

Love is a gift from the hand of God. He gives the love between a man and a woman, and He can help you to love in the right way – without jealousy and without giving into temptation. Ask the Lord now to help you love someone in the right way.

FISHING FOR JESUS

"Come, follow Me," Jesus said, "and I will make you fishers of men." (Mark 1:17)

Jesus uses the image of fishing to tell us how important it is that we "catch" people. A fisherman puts bait on a fish hook, or he lets a net down the side of the boat and pulls the fish in like that. What he catches belongs to him.

How do we catch people for Jesus? We tell them about Him. We also tell them how wonderful it is to know Him and to follow Him, because He is the one who forgives our sins and will let us live in heaven with Him. When people hear this, many of them will come to Him.

The Lord uses people like you and me to bring others to Him so that they can belong to Him. Be a fisher of people today.

NOT EMPTY RELIGION

Even though you bring me burnt offerings ... I will not accept them.
(Amos 5:22)

God does not like it when someone pretends to worship Him, but is not sincere. He does not like religion that is nothing but show. Some people seem to be children of God. They listen to sermons; they sing and look God-fearing. Yet they don't mean it.

Israel was like this. They sinned so much and didn't really love God. God said, "What good is your religion if you are not in a proper relationship with Me?" The Lord looks into our hearts. He knows if we confess our sins. He knows if we are forgiven. If we serve Him thankfully and go to church and sing Him songs, He is pleased with us. But He does not like an empty religion.

Work on your relationship with the Lord, and serve Him wholeheartedly.

A FATHER FOREVER

And He will be called ... Everlasting Father.
(Isaiah 9:6)

Some kids never see their fathers. Others might not even know who their father is. Some kids have fathers that treated them badly and left them.

No matter what our earthly father is like, we have a Heavenly Father who will always be there. He is the Father of Jesus, and He also becomes our Father when we accept Jesus. Jesus shows us the way to the Father. He introduces us to His Father. His Father becomes your Father and mine. He is a Father who will never disappoint us, who never makes mistakes, who will never turn His back on us, who will never leave us. Jesus saw to it that we have an everlasting Father.

God is with you today and He loves you.

EMPTY CLOUDS

*Like clouds and wind without rain is a man
who boasts of gifts he does not give.*
(Proverbs 25:14)

The Bible says we are sometimes like clouds without rain. We are full of promise, but nothing happens. It is easy to make promises. People say they will do this or that, and then nothing comes of it. People even boast about things they will achieve and how they will do things for you.

Perhaps you have had friends like this: full of promises about what they want to do for you, but it ended there – with the promise. They are like empty clouds without any rain.

We must not be like empty clouds. What we say, we must do. People must be able to rely on us. Don't be quick to boast about what you are going to do. It is better to keep quiet and first do it.

HOLY TO THE LORD

On that day HOLY TO THE LORD will be inscribed on the bells of the horses, and the cooking pots in the LORD's house will be like the sacred bowls in front of the altar.
(Zechariah 14:20)

Wherever the Lord is, it is holy. This means in your bedroom, or in the kitchen, or in church, or at school.

Zechariah saw a vision of the words "Holy to the Lord" written on the bells of the horses. Also the cooking pots in the house of the Lord were to be sacred or holy. With this vision God said that the time had come where all things were equally holy to the Lord. Actually He was saying that all things we use can be instruments to glorify the Lord.

Let us make everything we work with every day, holy. Because everything belongs to the Lord.

RESPECT THE ELDERLY

Gray hair is a crown of glory; it is gained by living a godly life. (Proverbs 16:31, NLT)

Many children are impatient with old people. Some even make fun of old people because they can't move fast, or because they do things differently.

Do you realize that today's old people were once just as young as you are? As the years went by, they got older, and later they started getting weaker.

The Bible says the gray hair of old people is like a splendid crown they wear on their heads. Make time to speak to old people. If you still have a grandpa and a grandma, make sure you call them regularly, or write them a letter or email just to say you love them. Let's pray for all old people who live in homes for the elderly.

GOD'S PROMISES

They will pray day and night, continually.
Take no rest, all you who pray to the Lord.
(Isaiah 62:6, NLT)

God makes a lot of promises to us in the Bible. He promises to be with us, to always love us, to strengthen us, to guide us. Isaiah tells us in this verse that we must remind the Lord of the promises He made. It's not because God forgets that we have to remind Him. It is because we sometimes forget about the Lord's promises that we must remember them again and must repeat them to ourselves and to God. If we do that, we show that we really put our trust in Him and that we need Him.

Every time you are in a difficult situation, think about one of the Lord's promises. Make it your own, in faith. Thank God that His promises are also meant for you.

BAD LANGUAGE

But now you must rid yourselves of ... filthy language from your lips. (Colossians 3:8)

Whatever is in your heart comes out of your mouth. If your heart is not clean, it is much easier to speak dirty words. Swearing is a sign of a heart that has not yet been cleaned well enough.

When we give our hearts to God, His Holy Spirit comes to live in our hearts, and He can help us to get our language clean. I know many people who once used very bad language, but when they gave their hearts to the Lord, they did not want to do it anymore.

Many Christians have the problem of a bad word slipping out every now and again. But we can say we're sorry right away and ask God to help us so that we do not use that word again.

THE TRUE GOD

Though the nations around us follow their idols, we will follow the LORD our God forever and ever. (Micah 4:5, NLT)

There are many different religions in the world, and everyone believes his god is the real one. As Christians we believe in the God of the Bible. He is the Father of Jesus Christ, and He gave us His Holy Spirit to stay with us and teach us all about His will.

As Christians we know the Bible is correct. Micah said all nations may live in the name of their gods here on earth, but we will always live in the name of the Lord our God. Christians say it is not only in this life that we must have a God and bow down before Him, but above all, it is in eternity that we will live with Him.

It is the Lord God who lives in our hearts.

WHEN PARENTS DIVORCE

"Should a man be allowed to divorce his wife for just any reason? Let no one split apart what God has joined together."
(Matthew 19:3, 6, NLT)

A lot of parents divorce. Divorce makes it so that families no longer live together in love and harmony. Often children do not know where they fit in – with Dad or with Mom. God does not like divorce.

Sometimes something happens between moms and dads and their marriage breaks down and just gets worse and worse. Where there was love at first, there is now growing disagreement. It is sad.

Even if people divorce, however, the Lord will heal the hurt. He can also forgive all the sins that have been committed.

In Jesus we can always start again, make a new beginning. Let's pray for marriages and families and ask for the Lord's blessing on these.

THROWING STONES

"If any one of you is without sin, let him be the first to throw a stone at her." (John 8:7)

In this Scripture verse we read about a married woman who cheated on her husband. The Old Testament said if anyone committed this sin, then that person must be stoned to death.

Jesus knew that the woman was guilty, but He wanted to forgive her. Jesus said that the person who was without sin could pick up the first stone and throw it at her. No one could do that, because all of them had sin in their lives. Jesus looked at the woman and told her that He didn't condemn her, but that she should not sin anymore.

You and I cannot throw stones at others, or accuse them, because of all the sin in our own lives. Let's not judge others, but rather pray for them.

PROTECT HIS NAME

"You shall not misuse the name of the LORD your God." (Exodus 20:7)

The name of the Lord is holy. The Jews in the Old Testament felt so strongly about the name of the Lord that they did not say it, not even when they prayed. They were afraid to because to them God was too great and holy.

As a Christian you may cringe when you hear how people use the name of Jesus, or God the Father, carelessly. God's name is noble and holy, and it must be used only when we speak of Him respectfully.

If we hear someone misusing the name of the Lord, we must pray for that person. We must explain in a nice way that we love God and that His name is special to us. We must tell them that He is the God we worship.

HELPING OTHERS

"But a Samaritan came where the man was; and when he saw him, he took pity on him. He went to him and bandaged his wounds." (Luke 10:33-34)

Jesus told the story of the good Samaritan. He helped the man who robbers had attacked and left half dead. Some other people pretended not to see the hurt man. When the Samaritan saw him, he took pity on him and started taking care of his wounds.

There are many people who are in pain or who have problems. The Bible says we must not look the other way, but must try to help them. The Samaritan not only bandaged the man's wounds, he also helped him onto his own donkey and took him to an inn, where he paid so that the man could stay there until he was well. This is real love. You and I must do the same with people around us who need help.

THE HOUSE CHURCH

Greet also the church that meets at their house. (Romans 16:5)

After Jesus ascended to heaven, Christians would meet in people's houses. They had their meals together, prayed together, and talked about Jesus. They also read the letters Paul and others wrote them. In this way they encouraged one another, and their faith was strengthened. Today people get together in smaller groups in people's homes. These small groups are connected to large congregations, and they get together regularly to study the Bible, pray, and worship the Lord. They care for each other and support one another.

What a privilege to get together openly in one another's homes to worship the Lord and to praise Him. Pray for these groups all over the world. Fortunately, we don't have only churches where we can praise God. He is with us in our own homes.

WONDERFUL FRIENDS

Greet Priscilla and Aquila, my fellow workers in Christ Jesus. (Romans 16:3)

The Lord gave Paul wonderful Christian friends. Just like us, Paul needed close friends to support him and help him. In the letter to the Romans we read about quite a few of these friends.

Priscilla and Aquila were two of Paul's coworkers. They not only made tents with him, they also preached the gospel with him. Andronicus and Junias were two friends who became Christians before Paul did, and they were in prison with him. Apelles was another good friend of Paul's. Paul says of him that he was a reliable Christian friend.

There are many other names we could list, but it is clear that Paul was very thankful for all these friends who helped him to serve the Lord and follow Him. You and I should have friends like these.

TWO EARS, ONE MOUTH

Too much talk leads to sin. Be sensible and keep your mouth shut. (Proverbs 10:19, NLT)

There's a saying, "A person has two ears and only one mouth." This means we must listen twice as much as we speak. Unfortunately, the opposite is often true; we talk much more than we listen.

Proverbs 10 says if we speak a lot, sin very easily comes into our speech. It is with all this talking that we sometimes say the wrong thing. We must speak less and be careful of what we say. Then we are wise, and we leave less room for sin in our speech.

Remember that your tongue can cause you to sin. Be careful with it. Ask the Lord to help you speak less and listen more. Ask the Lord to help you so that when you do talk it will be wise words.

GOOD ADVICE

And He will be called Wonderful Counselor.
(Isaiah 9:6)

We can have all the knowledge in the world and still not know the right way to live. We need more than book learning; we need good advice. Although we can get good counsel from people, the best counsel comes from the Lord. That is why the Bible calls Jesus "Counselor." He is a wonderful Counselor who can advise you and me about all things in life.

The most important counsel He wants to give us is how to live successfully. To choose Jesus and to follow Him is to have a wonderful Counselor. He talks to us in His Word and counsels us in many things. His Holy Spirit also leads us in truth. If we follow the Lord's advice, we should be happy.

CHANGED BY GOD

James and his brother John (to them he gave the name Sons of Thunder).
(Mark 3:17)

James and John were two disciples that Jesus chose to follow Him. Jesus gave them a nickname *Boanerges*, which means "Sons of Thunder." It seems that James and John came from a family with quick tempers. They sounded almost like thunder. Many people are like thunder. They get angry and angrier still, and later they explode like a peal of thunder.

John is later mentioned as the disciple whom Jesus loved very much, and John also loved Jesus. It is John who writes that we must love one another in 1, 2, and 3 John. When you give your life to Jesus, a miracle takes place: He changes your negative characteristics to positive ones. The Sons of Thunder later on became the Sons of Love. Allow the Lord to change you.

A GOOD NAME

A good name is more desirable than great riches. (Proverbs 22:1)

A name is important, and that is why we must see to it that we do not lose our good name. You get a good name when you do good things. If you have a lovable nature, or you like helping others, people know you as a lovable and helpful person.

The same goes for a bad name. If you have become known as a person who does mean things, people link these things you do to your name.

The Bible says a good name is worth more than riches. Once you have lost your good name, it is very difficult to get it back again. How lucky you are that the Lord helps you to live in such a way that, even if you do make mistakes, people know you mean well.

DON'T LOSE HEART

Each helps the other and says to his brother, "Be strong!" (Isaiah 41:6)

It is easy to give up hope. If things do not work out the way we planned them, we easily just give up.

Some people are wonderful at giving others hope. They bring out the best in us. When we are downhearted, they notice our sadness and do something to lift us out of it.

When athletes run in a marathon many runners get tired and feel like giving up. But along the road there are thousands of people who encourage them and tell them they're doing well and that they will make it to the end.

God helps and encourages us through His Holy Spirit. He fills our hearts with hope and courage. He is there to support us when there is no one else to give us hope.

STREAMS OF WATER

"Whoever believes in Me, as the Scripture has said, streams of living water will flow from within him." (John 7:38)

Jesus once talked to a sinful woman. She was busy getting water from a well just outside the town where she lived. Jesus told her that if she drank ordinary water, she would get thirsty again, but if she drank the water that He would give, she would never get thirsty again.

The water the Lord gives becomes like a fountain inside of us. Jesus Himself is like water to you and me. If we believe in Him, we are filled. Our thirst for sense and meaning in our lives is satisfied. He fills our hearts with His living water.

Thank the Lord, right now, for His living water. If you are still thirsty, drink from the fountain that is Jesus Himself.

THE PERFECT LAMB

"Look, the Lamb of God, who takes away the sin of the world!" (John 1:29)

In the Old Testament people brought offerings to receive forgiveness for their sins and to thank the Lord for what He had done for them. They usually sacrificed a perfect lamb. God sent Jesus to earth to be sacrificed for our sins.

In the same way that the lambs in the Old Testament took away sin, Jesus as the Lamb of God had to take away our sins. When His blood flowed and He died, He was the sacrifice for your sins and mine.

Today we do not sacrifice lambs anymore because the Lamb of God, Jesus Christ, was the last and perfect sacrifice for sin. You just need to accept it, and you will also be free of the guilt of sin.

WHATEVER YOU DO

So whether you eat or drink or whatever
you do, do it all for the glory of God.
(1 Corinthians 10:31)

Paul says whenever we eat, drink, or whatever we do, it must be to the glory of God. When is something to the glory of God? When we do it the way Jesus would do it. When we do it in love. When we serve others by doing it. When we do it in such a way that it does not go against the Word and the will of God.

When we watch TV, eat, drink, or chat, we need to ask: "Would Jesus do it this way?" We must remember that the Lord is always with us. Will He like watching what we do, and what will He think of the way we talk? Let's make Jesus feel at home with us! Let's do everything to His glory.

A STRONG FAITH

For this very reason, make every effort to add to your faith. (2 Peter 1:5)

Faith is the beginning of our spiritual life. If we believe in Jesus, we start a new life with Him, and He leads us on a new road. As we walk this road with Him, He teaches us through His Word, and the Holy Spirit speaks with us deep in our hearts. As we learn new things, our faith grows and becomes richer.

Faith is like the foundations of a house. A house cannot stand strong and firm if the foundations have not been made very strong. Faith is a strong foundation for you and me. Only when our faith is strong can we start building our faith-home: our lives.

We must work hard to add to our faith good qualities: knowledge, self-control, perseverance and love for one another.

DRY BONES COME TO LIFE

"I will put My Spirit in you and you will live, and I will settle you in your own land."
(Ezekiel 37:14)

Ezekiel had a vision of a valley full of dry skeletons; the bones were so dry they were white. God explained that His people, Israel, were like dry bones. God would put flesh and muscles on the bones and cover them with skin, and then He would give them a spirit so that they could live again.

Often people are like skeletons. Although they are breathing, they have no real life, no spiritual life. If you do not believe in Jesus and have not been saved, you are spiritually dead, just like a skeleton.

Even Christians can be half-dead spiritually, like the people of Israel. Then we need revival: the Holy Spirit must refill our lives so that we can do God's will.

I WILL, BUT FIRST ...

"I will follow You, Lord; but first let me go back and say goodbye to my family."
(Luke 9:61)

When Jesus told a man that he should also follow Him, his answer was, "Lord, first let me ... " (verse 59). He had an excuse: I will follow you but first I must do something else. Yet another person said he had to go and say goodbye to his family.

The lesson is that we must not follow the Lord if we're not going to do it wholeheartedly. Of course we can go and say goodbye to our families, but Jesus knew this man was just making a poor excuse for not wanting to follow Him.

Do you perhaps also make excuses for not following the Lord with all your heart? I hope there aren't a lot of "buts" in your life.

WRITTEN IN HEAVEN

"However, do not rejoice that the spirits submit to you, but rejoice that your names are written in heaven." (Luke 10:20)

Jesus sent out seventy-two of His followers to heal people, and tell them about the kingdom of God.

They thought it was wonderful that the name of Jesus was so strong that even the demons left people when they were told to do so in the name of Jesus.

Jesus was glad that they saw how wonderful His name and His power was, but He said they should rather have been happy to know that their names were written in heaven. To witness miracles and the power of God is important, but it is more important to know that your relationship with God is good, and that your name is written in the Book of Life.

LIKE THE DEAD

When I saw Him, I fell at His feet as though dead. (Revelation 1:17)

On Patmos Jesus appeared to John through the Holy Spirit. Jesus wore a long robe with a golden sash around His chest. His hair was as white as snow. His face was like the sun shining in all its brilliance.

Although John loved the Lord and was on earth with Him, he said, "When I saw Him, I fell at His feet as though dead" (verse 17). He was completely overwhelmed by the appearance of Jesus. But Jesus touched Him with His right hand, and said, "Do not be afraid. I am the First and the Last. I am the Living One" (verse 17, 18).

One day you will also see Jesus in all His glory. You don't have to be afraid. He will be loving toward us.

HIS GREATEST WISH

So we make it our goal to please Him.
(2 Corinthians 5:9)

We all have our dreams and goals for our lives. Paul was an ordinary person like us, but when Jesus changed his life, his dreams and goals became new. His most important wish was that his life would please the Lord.

This is a beautiful goal. If you live to please the Lord, you will be happy and will always have peace in your heart. Then there is also the Lord's promise: if we do His will and seek His kingdom, He will give us everything we need.

In Psalm 37:4 we read, "Delight yourself in the LORD and He will give you the desires of your heart." So, we see that Paul's greatest wish was to please the Lord, and what a great wish to have!

IT WAS NIGHT

Abram fell into a deep sleep, and a terrifying darkness came down over him.
(Genesis 15:12, NLT)

One night it became dark for Abram; not only outside, but also in his heart. A thick and terrifying darkness came over him. He must have worried about his life and his future. Often it is in the dark of night that we start worrying about things that can happen to us.

Just when Abram's fear was becoming too much for him to bear, God started talking to him. The Lord promised that He would be with him and would help him in everything he did. Sometimes when things are at their darkest in our lives, God wants to comfort us and tell us that He is with us and that He will keep His promises for our lives. Trust Him. As He cared for Abram, He will care for us.

FIRST MAKE PEACE

"Leave your gift there in front of the altar.
First go and be reconciled to your brothers;
then come and offer your gift."
(Matthew 5:24)

I n Jesus' time people brought offerings to
the altar. With these offerings they wanted
to make sure that they would always have a
good relationship with God.

You and I also bring the Lord offerings.
We go to church to worship Him. We give
money to thank Him for taking care of us.

Jesus tells us that we must first sort out
all bad feelings between us and someone
else before we offer Him anything. Often
when we are in God's presence, He reminds
us of something in our hearts that we have
against another person. Then we must stop
what we are doing and go and make our
peace with that person. Then we can bring
the Lord an offering.

THE BABY MOVED

When Elizabeth heard Mary's greeting, the baby leaped in her womb, and Elizabeth was filled with the Holy Spirit. (Luke 1:41)

When Mary was pregnant with Jesus, she went to visit her cousin Elizabeth. Elizabeth was also expecting a baby. That baby would later be known as John the Baptist.

As Mary greeted Elizabeth, the baby leaped inside her. It was a joyful movement, almost as if the baby inside Elizabeth was pleased that Jesus had come with Mary. At that moment, Elizabeth was filled with the Holy Spirit, and she started praising the Lord for the miracle of Jesus' coming birth.

If an unborn baby could react so wonderfully to the Savior, we should also be filled with great joy. We must glorify and praise the Lord with our mouths and with everything we do.

HE BRINGS PEACE

And He will be called ... Prince of Peace.
(Isaiah 9:6)

When Isaiah prophesied that Jesus would be born, he said that one of His names would be "Prince of Peace."

Peace is the opposite of war. When people make peace, they are not angry with one another anymore, and they no longer fight. It is good to live in peace. God wants us to live in peace with Him, and this is only possible if Jesus makes us free from sin.

Jesus is our Prince of Peace because He makes peace with God on our behalf, through the Holy Spirit.

The Lord helps us to live in peace with others. That is why the Bible calls the children of the Lord "peacemakers."

Thank the Lord that He came to bring peace in our hearts: peace with God, peace with others, and peace with ourselves.

A WICKED KING

He gave orders to kill all the boys ... who were two years old and under.
(Matthew 2:16)

The devil knew that Jesus would be born to become the Savior of humankind.

One of the things the devil did to try and put a stop to Jesus' plan of redemption was to work in the heart of King Herod. When Herod heard that someone had been born who would become a king, he decided immediately that this child had to be killed. So he gave orders to kill every baby boy born in and around Bethlehem within two years. Fortunately, an angel warned Joseph so that they could flee with Baby Jesus.

The devil will also try to ruin God's plans for your life, but God is stronger than the devil, and He will protect you. Just put your trust in Him.

A SMALL TOWN

"But you, Bethlehem Ephrathah, though you are small ... out of you will come for Me one who will be ruler over Israel." (Micah 5:2)

Long before Jesus was born, Micah prophesied that He would be born in Bethlehem. Bethlehem was a small town and not at all important.

Two things about this fact are important. The first is that Jesus was prepared to come to the humblest place on earth so that even the humblest person could know Jesus is not too good or too important to follow.

The second meaning of Jesus' birth in Bethlehem is that it did not happen by chance. God never makes a mistake. His prophecies always come true.

Praise the Lord because He was prepared to be an ordinary baby for your sake and mine, to be born in an ordinary place as God had prophesied.

OUR STRONG GOD

And He will be called ... Mighty God.
(Isaiah 9:6)

Nobody is as strong and powerful as God, the Father of Jesus Christ. He made the whole world. And He makes sure that everything is kept up. He is the great, strong, mighty God.

Isaiah prophesied that Jesus would also show the might of His Father. One of Jesus' names is "Mighty God." Jesus came to show God's power when He not only lived on earth and performed many miracles, but also when He died on the cross and afterward powerfully rose from the dead. When you and I are afraid, we are comforted by the thought that we have Someone with us who is strong and who can help us. God is always prepared to be with us. Trust in Him. He is also your mighty God. Ask Him to help you today.

THE GREATEST GIFT

"For God so loved the world that He gave His one and only son." (John 3:16)

A gift is something we are given for free. The best gifts are those we don't expect; someone loves us so much that they want to give us a present.

Christmas is that time of year when we give one another presents because we want to remember that God loved us so much that He gave us the best gift of all. The Lord looked at us and saw that we needed Him very much. Someone had to come and help us so that we would not perish in our sins. That is why the Father sent His Son. Everyone who believes in Him will have everlasting life, and there is no gift in heaven or on earth as great as this one.

Thank the Lord right now for the wonderful gift of Jesus!

GOD LIKES US

"On earth peace to men on whom His favor rests." (Luke 2:14)

When baby Jesus was born, an angel appeared to the shepherds near Bethlehem. And the angel said to them, "Do not be afraid. I bring you good news of great joy that will be for all the people. Today ... a Savior has been born to you ... This will be a sign to you: You will find a baby wrapped in cloths." (vv. 10-12). Suddenly millions of angels appeared, praising God and singing, "Glory to God in the highest, and on earth peace to men on whom His favor rests" (verse 14).

The angels praised the Lord because Jesus would bring peace on earth. Anyone who accepts Jesus as Lord finds peace because their sins have been forgiven. Peace is the Lord's Christmas gift to us because His favor rests on us.

I'M AVAILABLE

"I am the Lord's servant," Mary answered.
"May it be to me as you have said."
(Luke 1:38)

The angel Gabriel told Mary she would become pregnant and would have a baby boy, Jesus, who would be called the Son of the Most High and that He would reign as King forever. Mary was very surprised. She wanted to know how that was possible. He answered that the Holy Spirit would perform a miracle so that Jesus' life would start inside her body. God can do anything; nothing is impossible to Him. Then Mary said she was available to God and that He could do with her as He pleased.

How wonderful it is if you can tell God that you are available, that He can do with you anything He wants to. You can be a wonderful instrument for Him to use, just like Mary.

DECEMBER 25

IT'S CHRISTMAS!

"Today in the town of David a Savior has been born to you; He is Christ the Lord."
(Luke 2:11)

Today is Christmas Day! It is one of the most wonderful and most important days of the year.

Today we remember that Jesus was born a little baby in a manger in Bethlehem. He did not stay a baby. Jesus grew up and said He was the Redeemer. He also proved it by dying on a cross for you and me. There He paid the price for our sins. He is also the Lord, because He rose from the dead: "Lord" means He reigns as king over all the powers of darkness.

I hope you will have a very blessed Christmas and that it will be a wonderful day for you. Praise Jesus for being willing to come to this world as our Savior.

GOODWILL TO ALL

Let your gentleness be evident to all.
(Philippians 4:5)

The word *gentle* means kind, careful, not violent, merciful, sweet-tempered, willing. We are open to others, willing to meet them halfway. Friendly people are easy-going, open, loving, and considerate. How our country needs people like this!

There are many people in our country who don't like each other one bit. They make fun of each other, and they say bad things about each other. We have so many different cultures in our country yet we sometimes don't know members of another group. This means that we are not open to them. We are sometimes unfriendly toward others and sometimes even afraid of each other. We need goodwill.

Decide that wherever you go you will be friendly toward everybody, even if you don't know them.

MARANATHA

Come, Lord Jesus. (Revelation 22:20)

Christians are people who belong to Jesus, and they love the Lord. They would like to see Him and be with Him. I don't know about you, but I would love to be with Jesus one day – not only in faith, but really with Him, in His presence. The first disciples were very sad when He went up to heaven. They were sad because they didn't want Him to go away from them. In the very last verses of the Bible we find the words, spoken longingly, "Come, Lord Jesus!" (This is what "Maranatha" means.)

Jesus said that He will definitely come. Perhaps it will be soon. Let us be ready when He comes to get us. Until then, our hearts are longing for that day. Tell Him now that you are longing to see Him and that it will be wonderful to be with Him.

TOGETHER IN HEAVEN

"The rich man died and he looked up and saw Abraham." (Luke 16:22, 23)

The Bible says that we will recognize each other in heaven. When the rich man died, he recognized Abraham. We will also recognize our loved ones in heaven. If there is someone in your family who has died and is with Jesus, you will see each other again. Perhaps you will sit and talk for ages, because there is no such thing as time in heaven.

It is wonderful to know that one day we will be with our loved ones again in heaven. It seems to me that people will also see one another in hell, but there won't be time for anything good because of all the pain and suffering. I hope you belong to the Lord and that you are on your way to heaven.

THE COURT OF GOD

"The court was seated, and the books were opened." (Daniel 7:10)

At the end of the world everybody will appear before the great white throne of God. There we will all have to account for our lives. All those who do not believe in Jesus Christ will be judged. They will be found guilty of sin.

But Jesus is our great Advocate. His blood will cover our sins. We will not be punished – not because we did not sin, but because Jesus paid for our sins. It is so wonderful to know that you and I will walk out, free, because of Jesus. That is why our relationship with Jesus is so important. Have you asked Him to forgive your sins? Have you accepted His death on the cross as payment for your sins? He will pronounce you "not guilty" on Judgment Day. Thank God now because He is good.

THE TRUMPET CALL

"And He will send His angels with a loud trumpet call, and they will gather His elect."
(Matthew 24:31)

In the old days a trumpet was blown so that people knew something important was about to be said.

The Lord says there will be a loud trumpet call on the day Jesus comes back to earth. The Bible tells us that when the trumpet sounds, Jesus will appear in the sky. Everybody will see Him come with power and great glory. Then He will send His angels out to gather everyone who loves Him and knows Him, from all over the world. They will then live with Him forever.

Won't it be absolutely wonderful to see the Lord coming on the clouds? I think people who don't know Him will be very scared. You and I must be ready for Him when He comes again.

EBENEZER

He named it Ebenezer, saying, "Thus far has the Lord helped us." (1 Samuel 7:12)

The Israelites were at war with the Philistines and only God could save them. Samuel pleaded with the Lord for Israel, and He answered his prayers.

The Lord sent loud thunder, which threw the Philistines into such a panic that they could do nothing against Israel. Then Samuel set up a stone like a monument. He acknowledged that God helped them.

At the end of this year, we can look back and say the Lord has helped us. He helped and encouraged us with our schoolwork and in everything we did. Tell your family and friends, "Up until now, the Lord has helped me." If we know the Lord was with us during this past year, we can look ahead and know that this same Lord will also be willing to be with us in the new year.